A Guidebook for Today's Asian Investor

Bruce VonCannon

A Guidebook for Today's Asian Investor

The Common Sense Guide to Preserving Wealth in
a Turbulent World

Bruce VonCannon
Vanheel Management Ltd
Central, Hong Kong

ISBN 978-981-10-5830-1   ISBN 978-981-10-5831-8   (eBook)
https://doi.org/10.1007/978-981-10-5831-8

Library of Congress Control Number: 2017955045

Cover illustration: © KeithBishop / DigitalVision Vectors / Getty Images

Printed on acid-free paper

This Palgrave imprint is published by Springer Nature
The registered company is Springer Nature Singapore Pte Ltd.
The registered company address is: 152 Beach Road, #21-01/04 Gateway East, Singapore 189721, Singapore

PREFACE

This book is devoted to the thousands of young hardworking adults who through their efforts are moving forward in their lives each day providing for the wellbeing of the ones they love. Today as this book goes to press there are approximately 15 million millionaires in the world. That number is growing at a pace of about 6% per year. That is, at its current pace, an additional 900,000 new millionaires are being created globally each year. They are growing in every country and community in the world where there is high level of industriousness and thriftiness. Estimates are that in the coming five years, another four and a half million millionaires will be created. I am convinced that our society today, hardly perfect and really deficient in many ways, benefits enormously from millionaires and those who aspire to achieve great wealth. It is wealth in the free markets that allows more choice in lifestyle, more choice and influence in how our political leaders are selected and lead, and creates higher likelihood for better educational standards, health standards, and breakthroughs in science and technology. When man is poor, his choices are limited. When man creates wealth, the tide of opportunity for himself and those around him rise in tandem.

This book is also devoted to the corps of private bankers and wealth managers around the world who each day try to do their best to offer good advice and wise counsel to their clients. In recent years, it has become fashionable to trash bankers and wealth managers. No doubt the economic downturn in 2008 had an impact on how many in our society view banks and financial institutions. In the post-2008 period, I became dismayed over how negative the rhetoric towards bankers became. In my nearly 30 years of experience, I feel just the opposite about the character and integrity of most private bankers and wealth managers. I know the majority of them to be very honest and hardworking and put their clients' interests first and foremost each day. My good friend, Pascal Bourqui, with whom I worked so closely in the industry for 20 years, once called the majority of our work colleagues "pearls in a necklace." While society today often venerates and creates hype for superstars, Pascal promoted the concept of a team that was comprised of individuals who more closely resembled pearls rather than diamonds. Diamonds no doubt are often beautiful pieces of jewelry and surely standout. However, Pascal as our team leader always encouraged us to see ourselves as pearls (rather than diamonds) because a pearl tends to look better when paired together with other pearls like in a necklace. Pearls exhibit the qualities of blending in with the team to create superior quality through teamwork, high level of trust, and loyalty to fellow staff and clients.

Finally, this book is intended to be a practical guide for persons who really want to understand the important fundamentals of managing one's wealth. If I have done my work correctly, you do not necessarily need to have a college degree to understand the concepts that I have introduced here. This book is intended to be suitable for reading by everyone young or old. It is also intended to be a book for those who have inherited wealth from loving parents, a relative, or friend or for those who are self-made. It is also for those just starting to build a nest egg and want their savings to expand and grow over time. While I think some of the underlying principles in this book are possibly scholarly, it is intended to be understood by all. Basically, as long as you can read and whether age 16 or 96, this book is for you. I will only offer one warning: If you are reading this book in order to derive a "get rich quick" secret, then please go ahead and throw it in the trash basket or trade it in at a book mart for another book. One thing I have learned about accruing great wealth is that there are few (if any) "get rich quick" gimmicks for wealth accumulation. Aside from those who inherit wealth, the vast majority of wealthy persons who accumulate great wealth do so because they work hard and stay committed to a way of life that abets saving and wealth accumulation. So, if you are reading this book to pick up on some successful methods for understanding the financial markets and using them to your advantage, then I advise you to keep this book nearby your nightstand or morning coffee cup. I and my fellow work "pearls" invite you to read on!

Acknowledgements

I have been blessed in my lifetime by many good people and some really great mentors. I should start by thanking my parents, the late E. J. "Buddy" VonCannon Jr. and Doris Hoffman Allred, for providing the appropriate environment for growing up in Piedmont North Carolina and always emphasizing education. They both grew up in the Great Depression in the 1930s as salt of the earth people experiencing the cruelty of economic hardship and the challenge of growing up with limited access to higher education. They passed along a lot of love and encouragement to me and my sisters and ensured a pathway to higher education.

I should also thank many other mentors that I had in my younger years. They included the late Morris Whitson, Jim Leighton, and my college tennis coach, Dave Benjamin, who through his role modeling taught us the importance of education and how it might shape our lives in the future after the halcyon days of university life.

My career in finance and wealth management started later than many as I was not one to rush to Wall Street immediately after graduating from university in the rebellious days after the Vietnam War in the 1970s. Nor was I one that would have overly impressed anyone with my knowledge of financial theory in the novice stages of my career in banking and finance. Whatever success I achieved later in my career was in large part due to some good breaks that occurred as I hunkered down and just tried to do my job well. My work career was greatly abetted by the encouragement of people like Sandy Trentham, who early on taught me many social skills in the business world; by Ben Moyer and Jim Vaughn who placed great faith in me and gave me chances to advance my career when (frankly) not many others might have thought it justifiable to do so.

I thank a few other great personal friends, General Ma Kan, Howard Brewer and Faye Angevine, and H.C. Tang for their philosophical and intellectual exchange over the years. Many thanks to Sumi and Anna Chang and their sons Daniel and Simon for their personal friendship and professional guidance over the years as well as Harald VanHeel and Cindy Leung whose humor, wisdom, and enthusiasm I have appreciated over coffee each morning as we review the overnight markets.

I also thank so many of my Swiss colleagues with whom I worked for many years in Asia and Geneva. For the most part, they were consummate professionals. If ever one business culture does not venerate superstars, it is the Swiss corporate culture that places a high premium on team work, consensus decision making, sharing credit and glory, and doing so without drawing so much attention to oneself. Within this cluster of close friends, I thank Balz Kloti, Marcel Kreis, Bernard Schaub, Pascal Bourqui, and Nick Ng. I also pay tribute to some of the finest women that I have worked with in this industry including Bella Lee, Judy Lee, Ping Yang, Theresa Tobias, Jennifer Lui, and Annie Tam.

Thanks would not be complete without thanking my beautiful and loving wife, SanSan, who has remained steadfastly behind me all these years through the peaks and valleys of my personal odyssey and business career. One of my favorite private banking clients once joked to me that my greatest accomplishment was probably being married to her—something I have come to mostly agree with after our 35 years of marriage! I also thank our two children, Max and Tiffany, who have been the most wonderful children that a parent could ever ask for.

I also wish to cite the extraordinary support and assistance of those who played a critical role in helping me bring this book to completion. These persons include Frank Lavin, a consummate business leader, diplomat, and strategic advisor who was a towering beacon of guidance on the finer points of authorship. Words of gratitude are due to Dan Kadison whose psychological and legal tips were helpful. I thank Mindy Hsu, who patiently and tirelessly helped me early on with research and formatting; Tom Pyle, a great friend who was always available for a quick phone call and 360 degree perspective on just about any topic; Ed Tiryakian, a true scholar who exhorted me to reach deeper and challenged me to seek a higher degree of excellence; Bill Lunsford, one of my oldest friends dating back to childhood for his outstanding artistic assistance preparing many of the cartoons and illustrations in this book; Yves Pflieger, French author and family friend since my youth; and Max VonCannon, my son, who helped me on editing and meeting publisher requirements and deadlines and Tiffany VonCannon, my daughter, who gave me many artistic suggestions. Thanks also to Anne Depaulis, a wealth management colleague in Geneva many years ago and a fine author in her own right, who greatly inspired me with her writings. I would like to say a word of gratitude to Carter Wrenn, a savant without peer, who gave me the clue that when humored all people follow the story line and Boyd Sturges, a great legal mind, who has always had my back.

As the great English philosopher Sir Isaac Newton once said, "If I can see afar it is because I have sat on the shoulders of giants." I know this is true in every sense.

Bruce VonCannon

CONTENTS

LIST OF FIGURES

CHAPTER 1

Understanding the Money Markets

> **Did You Know?**
> The first known private bankers originated in the seventeenth century from the modern-day Swiss Alps region following the Revocation of the Edict of Nantes by French King Louis XIV in 1685. Previously this edict had mandated religious freedom on French soil. However, after its revocation non-Catholics began annual treks into the mountainous Alps region of Europe near modern-day Geneva to store their wealth with reliable and trustworthy money merchants in exchange for a fee!

Part of building a framework of understanding in the investment world is to understand the three major asset classes: cash and money market products, bond and fixed income instruments, and equity products. There is a lot more to understand, too. However, in the beginning of an effort to acquire an understanding of the global financial markets, it is helpful to form a picture framework of the financial world by starting with these three asset classes.

Let's talk first about cash and the money markets.

The characteristics of cash and the money markets that should be important to you include the following.

© The Author(s) 2017
B. VonCannon, *A Guidebook for Today's Asian Investor*,
https://doi.org/10.1007/978-981-10-5831-8_1

It is where you place funds that you might need to use in the short term (i.e. within the next 12 months).

You should have realistic and I might say limited expectations of what level of return you can expect to receive in return for depositing your funds.

When placing your cash funds in any institution, you should pay just as much attention to the safety of the institution as to the return that is being offered. In fact, an offered return significantly above the market average should be a red flag or warning sign and prompt you to at least make routine inquiries about the safety of the institution that is taking your deposit funds.

The following investment products would normally be included in the category of money market products:

cash deposits
time deposits
certificates of deposit (CDs)
money market funds

What are your risks investing in these products?

Before 2008 one would probably say there is little or no risk investing in money market products. However, when the US and global financial system nearly imploded in 2008, institutional risk became much more of a concern than at anytime during the past 80 years (Fig. 1.1).

How is the investor protected against such risk? For years the US government offered up to USD 100,000 Federal Depository Insurance Corporation (FDIC) protection for any investor placing cash deposits in a US domiciled bank. Since 2008, that amount has actually been raised to USD 250,000. The FDIC states that depositors at an FDIC-insured bank that has gone into bankruptcy can expect to receive their money back up to USD 250,000 within two days after the institution has been declared a failed institution assuming the depositors have proper documentation validating their deposits.

Recently in the Peoples Republic of China, Chinese financial authorities also enacted the first form of modern depositor insurance by setting a RMB 500,000 (approximately USD 80,000) deposit insurance guideline. In various countries around the world, some governments have also offered to protect the principal of cash deposited by investors in its banks. Singapore and Hong Kong are two notable locations where following the severe financial crisis in 2008, the banking authorities sought to protect any client placing cash deposits in their domiciled banks by guaranteeing deposits. Switzerland, where approximately one third of the world's off-

Fig. 1.1 "Whatever you do don't look, just keep on walking." Note: This figure is a pun designed to create humor around the theme of bank safety—you will note in the window a sign reading "Bank of Titanic."

shore wealth is stored, raised their guaranteed deposit level from Swiss Franc 25,000 to Swiss Franc 125,000 a few years ago as well.

I guess losing a significant portion of your wealth in event of your local bank becoming insolvent might induce you to consider placing cash under your mattress. However, if you do that you would miss out on the interest paid on cash deposits. So let's now talk a bit about the rates of return that are normally earned on deposits.

Up until about the year 2000 you could have probably expected to earn up to 4% per annum return on a US dollar time deposit (see Fig. 1.2). That means for every USD 1 million placed in deposit at a bank, you could have earned approximately USD 40,000 per year (or over USD 3,000 per month) in interest. The intention by most banks has traditionally been to offer a deposit rate that slightly exceeds inflation rate.

Many banks also offer money market funds as a comparable product to time deposits. They provide interest returns to investors that is similar (i.e. sometimes higher, sometimes lower) than short-term time deposit rates.

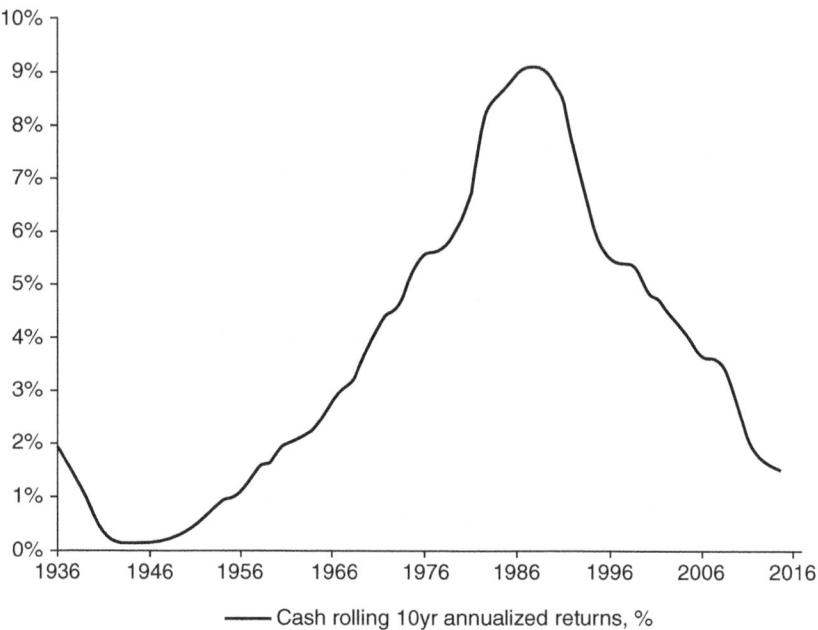

Fig. 1.2   Measuring US dollar cash returns since 1936 using 91 day US Treasury bills as a proxy for cash deposits. Note: This chart shows how dramatically USD short term interest deposits have fallen roughly since 2001.

They are typically attractive to investors who like to go in and out of the stock market frequently as they normally can be redeemed on 48 hours notice and free up cash more conveniently than a time deposit. However, the investor should bear in mind that money market funds while generally safe are not insured by FDIC insurance. In event the money market fund issuer goes into default, the investor can be left holding the bag! This actually occurred in 2008 when some investment banks (who were not allowed to be deposit taking institutions) lured investors into keeping their short-term cash in money market funds which became illiquid when the bank failed.

However, following the 9/11 terrorist attacks, the US Federal Reserve (or "the Fed" as we commonly call it) began an "accommodative" interest rate policy that resulted in US dollar three-month time deposit rates being currently quoted at less than 0.50% per annum. While short-term deposit rates began to move upward again by 2006 and 2007, the Great Financial Crisis (GFC) of 2008 resulted in rates plummeting again to near zero

1980	11.22%	1990	7.55%	2000	5.76%	2010	0.13%
1981	14.30%	1991	5.61%	2001	3.67%	2011	0.03%
1982	11.01%	1992	3.41%	2002	1.66%	2012	0.05%
1983	8.45%	1993	2.98%	2003	1.03%	2013	0.07%
1984	9.61%	1994	3.99%	2004	1.23%	2014	0.05%
1985	7.49%	1995	5.52%	2005	3.01%	2015	0.21%
1986	6.04%	1996	5.02%	2006	4.68%	2016	0.51%
1987	5.72%	1997	5.05%	2007	4.64%		
1988	6.45%	1998	4.73%	2008	1.59%		
1989	8.11%	1999	4.51%	2009	0.14%		

Fig. 1.3 3-Month Treasury Bill: Secondary Market Rate Source: Us Department of the Treasury

following Fed actions to stimulate the economy via ultra-accommodative monetary policy. Essentially the Fed's actions lowered the three-month interest rate to levels not seen for nearly a generation. Earning 0.50% per year on a USD 1 million deposit is approximately USD 5,000 per year (or just over USD 400 per month). That is significantly different from earning USD 3,333 per month as would be the case if US dollar short-term interest rates were (like pre-2000 levels) at 4.0% per annum.

The zero interest rate policy (also known by the acronym "ZIRP") of the US Federal Reserve (our Central Bank equivalent in the United States) has also had very significant impact on our country in recent years and many investors are increasingly becoming aware of it. The chart in Fig. 1.3 gives a recent historical record of the US dollar three-month Treasury bill rates which are within a comparable range of time deposit rates at many commercial banks. As you can see from the chart, following the 9/11 terrorist attacks in 2001 there was a dramatic shift downward in short-term US dollar rates. Conventional wisdom states that lower short-term rates serve to invigorate the economy when it is in the doldrums and stimulate consumption and investment activity.

Short-term rates are largely impacted by the monetary policy of the central bank of the United States which we call the US Federal Reserve (or commonly called in street jargon "The Fed"). Short-term rates stayed low during most of the first term of the George W. Bush presidency and started to rise again as economic conditions were improving. However, short-term rates spiked lower again in 2008 with the advent of the Global Financial Crisis and they became even lower during the Obama presidency. While the Chairman of the US Federal Reserve is appointed by the President of the United States, "The Fed" normally is empowered to act with independence in regard to how it conducts monetary policy.

Conducting a ZIRP policy is not something new that only recently happened starting after the 9/11 terrorist attacks and as a response to GFC in 2008. Zero rates have been seen in other countries for a long time. Japan is a country that has a history of deploying a ZIRP policy. Interest rates in Japan have been extraordinarily low for many, many years. Switzerland, in fact, introduced "negative interest rates" in the 1970s in order to (among other things) to weaken its currency. Negative yields on bonds started to occur in recent years in Europe as part of the extremely accommodative monetary policy of the European Central Bank under the leadership of Mario Dragi.

Some think a good test of a bank's safety is the Capital Adequacy ratio (CAR) which has been promoted by the Bank of International Settlements (BIS) based in Basel, Switzerland.

The BIS is a supra-national organization based in Switzerland set up in 1930 by eight Western democracies including the United States and Great Britain. It has served over the years to establish standards for transparency and safety in international banking. It serves central banks around the world promoting cooperation and monetary and financial stability.

CAR is also known as Capital to Risk (Weighted) Assets Ratio (CRAR) and is a measure of a bank's capital to its risk in the market. National regulators in the developed world track bank CAR in order to ensure that the banks can absorb a reasonable amount of loss and comply with the BIS capital requirements.

Bank capital is analyzed in a two-tier process:

Tier One capital: that is, a capital level that allows a bank to withstand losses without a bank being required to cease trading.

Tier Two capital: that is, a capital level that allows a bank to absorb losses in the event of a winding down activities and providing a lesser degree of protection to depositors.

Basically CAR is similar to leverage and can be compared to the inverse of a debt-to-equity leverage formula. CAR uses equity over assets instead of debt over equity. Also unlike conventional leverage ratios, CAR recognizes that assets can have different levels of risk. Specifics of CAR calculation may vary slightly from country to country, but they tend to be similar when assessed by BIS.

Currently under Basel III requirements, CAR for an international bank must be maintained at 8%.

Today most prominent big banks (e.g. Citibank, UBS, and Credit Suisse) maintain a CAR of approximately 11%. Curiously during the 2008 sub-prime crisis several of the big banks were in danger of going below 8% (the likes of whom included Citibank and UBS) and took emergency measures to re-capitalize amidst massive write-offs resulting from reckless sub-prime exposure.

Another common sense measure of a bank's safety is the bank's leverage ratio. The Basel III accords have defined a bank's leverage ratio as being "capital measure" over "exposure measure." "Capital measure" is essentially considered to be the bank's Tier 1 capital—recall earlier that we define it to be the capital level required to ensure that a bank can withstand losses without being required to cease trading. "Exposure measure," on the other hand, consists of four types of exposures: (1) on-balance sheet exposure, (2) derivative exposure, (3) securities financing transactions (SFT), and off-balance sheet (OBS) items.

The BIS has stated in its research reports in recent years that "an underlying cause of the GFC of 2008 was the buildup of excessive on- and off-balance sheet leverage in the banking system.

In recent years the asset growth in some of the very large banks has become so high and accordingly so highly leveraged that it has created concern at senior government levels that potential liabilities of the bank, in event of bankruptcy, would be beyond the ability of the government to come to the rescue. For example, two of the major Swiss banks in recent years had balance sheets so bloated that their level of assets exceeded the GDP of their home country. In event of a spate of bad loans they would not be possibly able to defend themselves and the impact on the country's financial system could potentially become catastrophic.

So, in response to a growing chorus of anti-bank sentiment across the developed nations of the world, regulators are working feverishly to regain the trust of the public who have endured a less than impressive set of behaviors during the past decade. US financial regulators have stipulated that leverage ratio for banks should be maintained at a 3% level.

In summary, understanding the money market instruments is important for building one's knowledge about investing. Many investors take for granted this asset class and consider it failsafe. History has shown this not to always be the case. Having a basic knowledge about the fundamental metrics of a bank's CAR and leverage ratio will help the investor to make wiser choices about where to deposit money. Understanding how FDIC insurance may or may not apply to deposit safety can be critical to protecting one's wealth as well. Finally, understanding that there may be a price to pay for just keeping one's cash under the mattress and earning no interest is basic to understanding investing (Fig. 1.4).

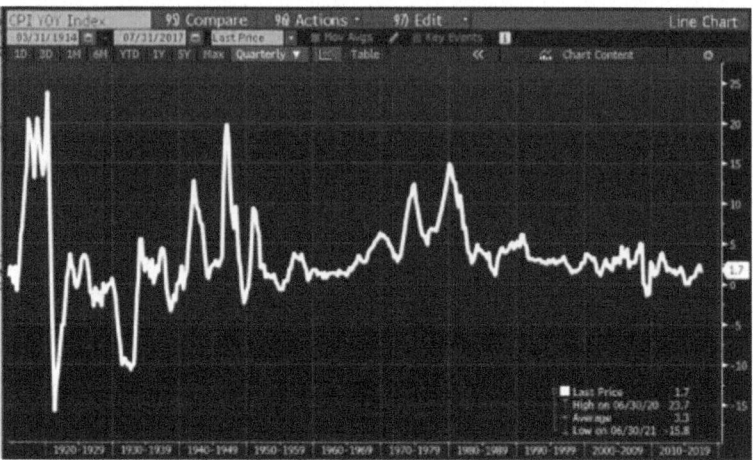

Fig. 1.4 U.S. Inflation Rate since 1914. Inflation is extremely low by historical standards. The trend of U.S. inflation is the lowest it has been since the 1960s. Low inflation rates across the globe in 2016 reflect the ongoing struggle to cope with the deflationary headwinds of excessive debt, de-leveraging, default risk, technological disruption, and demographic shifts.

CHAPTER 2

Understanding the Fixed Income Markets

Did You Know?
The first government bonds were issued in the Netherlands in 1517 when the city of Amsterdam issued long-term debt notes to finance infrastructure expansion. The bonds paid coupon interest to reward investors for their investment. Today the global bond market value is estimated in excess of USD 87 trillion and more than double in value to that of the global stock markets.

Fixed income instruments are another of the major asset classes that should be understood by investors. They are more commonly called "bonds" in the daily vernacular of the financial world and there are several types of bonds. For simplistic purposes for now let's just say that they (unlike time deposit or money market instruments) are an asset class that usually extend over a period lasting longer than time deposits and with a maturities that may be between 2 years lasting up to (in the case of US Treasury bonds) 30 years.

Also it is critical to understand that they are debt instruments, meaning they represent an obligation by the issuer (usually a government or a corporation) to borrow money for a period of time and pay a fixed or floating rate of interest until the bond expiry date when the bond must be repaid in full at its par (or issue) price. Sometimes a bond can be "called" or taken out of the market at a set price by the issuer and we call that a "callable

© The Author(s) 2017
B. VonCannon, *A Guidebook for Today's Asian Investor*,
https://doi.org/10.1007/978-981-10-5831-8_2

bond." Sometimes a bond issued by a corporation may be "converted" into the equity of a corporation by the buyer of the bond at a set price and we call that a "convertible bond."

In the private banking world it used to be the case that bonds were mainly the domain of wealthy, older people and institutional investors. Bonds as financial instruments were characterized by their reliable fixed return and persons of wealth could place funds into such market instruments and expect to receive a fixed (pre-determined) coupon payment payout on a set date. It was so reliable that they could then book their winter holiday trip to Boca Raton! Today bond coupon payment payouts are still on schedule, but the coupon payouts and derived yields on bonds have become lower and lower. It won't pay so easily for the winter holiday trip to Boca Raton! Nevertheless, bond instruments are still important to your investment knowledge and holding some exposure in your investment portfolio should be considered.

It is worth noting some of the developments in the bond market in the past 35 years. Some notable events have spiced up this area of investing. Michael Milken, a brilliant member of the US investment community, and some of his colleagues invented a niche in the financial markets called "junk bonds" back in the 1980s. (Note: Poor Milken, in 1989 he pleaded guilty to some securities and reporting violations related to his firm Drexel Burnham Lambert and was permanently barred from the securities community but not before making a really valuable contribution to modern finance.) Milken led an avant-garde movement in the securities industry that furthered economic growth in this country and freed up large amounts of capital that had been trapped in old-line businesses. He helped many investors to discover that, while junk bonds as a stand-alone instrument could be risky, taken in portfolio they could represent outstanding value in the high-yield universe of bond investing. To some people Michael Milken still today remains legend!

THE ARGUMENT FOR INVESTING IN FIXED INCOME INSTRUMENTS

Let's look at why you should pay attention to the bond markets. Normally, they offer higher returns than time deposits and money market instruments. For money that you have been keeping in your piggy bank or little nest egg that is not needed within the next 12 months, you should consider some exposure to the bond market. There are typically offerings with maturities ranging from 2 years up to 30 years. For individual investors, I suggest you focus on the maturities in the three- to ten-year range. Going beyond ten years tends to be an area more suited for life insurance companies than the average person!

The beauty of investing into bonds is that the wise investor may stand to gain a superior interest rate differential compared to a time deposit. Most of the time the yield curve for money of one year or less (i.e. time deposits) is higher as one goes out to two years, five years, ten years, and beyond. Unless we would be in an unusual market scenario, the yield and interest payment for a five-year bond will be higher than the yield on a three-month or six-month time deposit.

Another attractive aspect of bonds is that the investor may be able to lock in a capital gain if the price of a bond increases, which normally happens when interest rates might fall for a specific time maturity. In fact, even when an investor might buy a ten-year bond, it is the case more often than not that the investor will trade or sell off the bond if a capital gain opportunity occurs.

As a bond approaches maturity, its price will gravitate closer and closer towards par value (or 100). This may be helpful to remember particularly before you buy a bond trading at a premium (that is, trading at a price above the price of 100). While you may gain some positive cash flow on a high coupon bond and over the long run have a positive Yield to Maturity, if you have bought the bond at a premium and hold it to maturity, then you will receive less in principal than you had invested when the bond matures. So pay attention and beware whether or not you are buying a bond at a premium (above par price) or at a discount (below par price).

A common and sometimes mistaken assumption about interest rate and bond yields is that the longer the maturity of the debt instrument, the higher the rate of interest will be. This is only partially true. It will serve you well to understand the importance of the "yield curve" in relation to the bond markets. The yield curve is also referred to as the "term structure of interest rates." It is essentially charts the interest rates paid or yield on bonds of various maturities across different contract maturities whether it be 1 month, 3 months, 5 years, 10 years, or even up to 30 years. One might assume that the rate for investing or borrowing for 3 months will be lower than the rate for 30 years. Under what is called a "normal yield curve" that is correct. However, there are moments in financial history where the yield curve may become a "flat yield curve," meaning that rates are almost identical regardless the tenor of the investment or borrowing.

Fig. 2.1 The normal yield curve

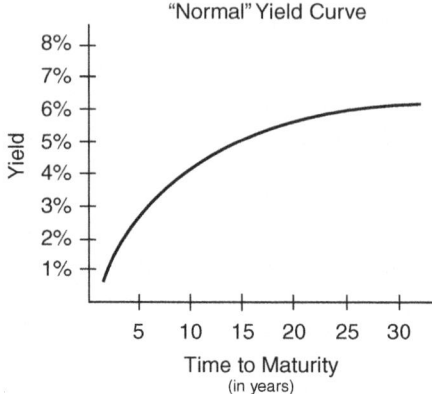

Fig. 2.2 The flat yield curve

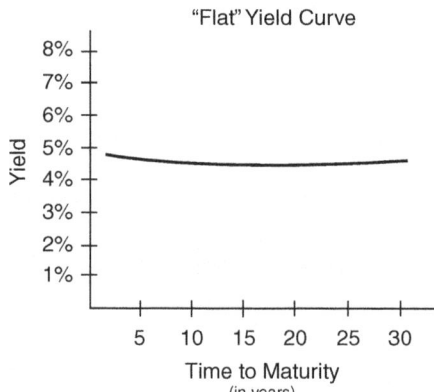

There are also more extreme oddities in the history of the yield curve when the phenomenon of an "inverted yield curve" occurs. An inverted yield curve is normally associated with a severe slowdown in the economy and actually occurred in 2008 on the eve of the Great Financial Crisis. For more on "yield curves" kindly see attached Figs. 2.1, 2.2, and 2.3.

A "normal" yield curve is normally associated with a healthy economy. The yield on long-term bonds is slightly higher than on short-term bills. A much steeper yield curve than what appears in the illustration would be expected if long-term rates are much higher than short-term rates and would suggest that investors are anticipating rapid economic growth. Such yield curve scenario existed in mid-2005 about three and

Fig. 2.3 The inverted yield curve

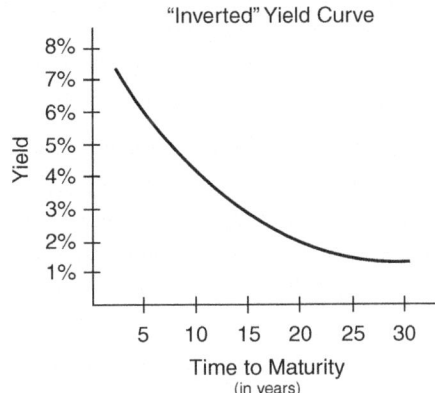

a half years after the 9/11 terrorist attacks when the US economy was starting to expand again.

A "flat" yield curve normally occurs when short-term rates edge higher and longer term rates fall. An example of this occurred in late 2015 when the US Fed raised short-term rates by 0.25%. It pushed up the short-term yields on the graph above. However, long-term rates which are determined by the market, actually fell and implied that rates might remain low in the future.

When short-term rates actually rise above long-term rates, investors would label it an inverted yield curve environment. Such scenario usually is a sign of imminent recession as long-term rates are an estimation of the outlook for shorter term instruments. Falling long-term rates imply that there will be a future decline in short-term rates. It suggests a weakening of the economic environment. Inversion occurred in 2000 and 2006–2007 and in both instances were followed by economic recession. In fact, 48% of global yield curves were inverted at the time of the Global Financial Crisis (GFC) in 2008.

RISKS IN THE BOND MARKETS

There are various types of bond instruments such as corporate bonds, government bonds, convertible bonds, zero coupon bonds, inflation-linked bonds, and floating rate bonds. There is risk associated with any type of investment instrument out there and here are the key risks that I think you should be aware of when investing in bonds.

Credit Ratings and Issuer Risk

Some issuers are safer than others. One way to dissect the level of risk is by looking at the credit rating of the issued bond or the issuer. There are currently three major internationally recognized credit rating agencies in the world today. They are Moody's, Standard and Poor's, and Fitch Ratings. The Chinese have also developed bond rating agencies in recent years. One is called China Chenxin International Credit Rating Co. (CCXI) which is a joint venture with Moody's Investor Service. The other Chinese rating agencies include China Lianhe Credit Rating Co. Ltd. (a joint venture with Fitch), Shanghai Brilliance Credit Rating & Investors Service (a joint venture with Standard and Poor's), and two other independent agencies called Dagong Global Credit Rating Co. Ltd. and Shanghai Far East Credit Rating Co. Ltd. Essentially these organizations provide helpful knowledge to the investment community as they essentially rate fixed instruments traded in the market in a similar fashion when it comes to rating the quality of the risk.

For convenience, let's use Moody's terminology for comparing credit ratings (bearing in mind we could have also used the slightly different credit rating metrics used by the other rating agencies as well). So the safest Moody's credit rating would be AAA but today there are only a handful of governments, banks, and corporations that have AAA credit rating. You will find the vast majority of investment worthy bonds are rated AA, A, or BBB. Once a bond is rated below BBB, it is called a "junk bond" and its risk of default is considered to be distinctly higher than a bond which has investment grade status. Investors sometimes ponder the wisdom of whether or not to invest in a junk bond. It has been my experience that conservative investors should avoid the risk of bonds with such a rating. However, if one's risk appetite is aggressive and one does not tie up too substantial an amount of one's wealth into such type of bond, then there are numerous examples of investors who have gained handsome returns investing in what is often called the "high-yield" bond market that may include some bonds with junk rating status (Fig. 2.4).

An aberration in the junk bond market occurred in 2007 as some investment banks were increasingly packaging junk bonds into bundled packages of bonds called "collateralized debt obligations" (CDOs). In numerous instances, the credit rating agencies were negligent in their credit rating of these instruments sometimes giving them inflated investment grade ratings (e.g. A, BBB) and masking the real risk of default. A lot of these CDOs

Credit ratings, following the definitions and methodology of credit rating agencies

	Moody's	S&P	Fitch/ I BCA	Credit rating definition
Investment grade	Aaa	AAA	AAA	Obligations rated Aaa are judged to be of the higher quality, with minimal credit risk.
	Aa1 Aa2 Aa3	AA+ AA AA-	AA AA-	Obligations rated Aa are judged to be of high quality and are subject to very low credit risk.
	A1 A2 A3	A+ A A-	A+ A A-	Obligations rated A are considered upper medium grade and are subject to low credit risk.
	Baa1 Baa2 Baa3	BBB+ BBB BBB-	BBB+ BBB BBB-	Obligations rated Baa are subject to moderate credit risk. They are considered medium grade and as such may possess certain speculative characteristics.
Non-investment grade	Ba1 Ba2 Ba3	BB+ BB BB-	BB+ BB BB-	Obligations rated Ba are judged to have speculative elements and are subject to substantial credit risk.
	B1 B2 B3	B+ B B-	B+ B B-	Obligations rated B are considered speculative and are subject to high credit risk.
	Caa1 Caa2 Caa3	CCC+ CCC CCC-	CCC+ CCC CCC-	Obligations rated Caa are judged to be of poor standing and are subject to very high credit risk.
	Ca	CC C	CC+ CC CC-	Obligations rated Ca are highly speculative and are likely in, or very near, default, with some prospect of recovery of principal and interset.
	C	D	DDD	Obligations rated C are the lowest rated class of bonds and are typically in default, with little prospect for recovery of principal or interset.

Fig. 2.4 Credit ratings: following the definitions and methodology of the major credit rating agencies

were re-packaged mortgages in the United States housing market that had limited chance of ever being repaid. The acronym "CDO" has become almost a dirty word in the industry because of this dark period of real estate financing in the United States. The role of rating agencies in international finance following the 2008 crisis also came under intense scrutiny as there were numerable instances where investment grade companies went into default, and shareholders and clients holding their obligations were punished. As the dust clears from the damage to the global economy and everyday mainstreet investors following the 2008 crisis, such criticisms have brought about changes in how the big three rating agencies (Moody's, Standard and Poor's, and Fitch) conduct their activities and hopefully resulted in heightened standards in the years.

It is worthwhile to review the likelihood of unpleasant outcomes even when one is staying within the investment grade area of the bond world.

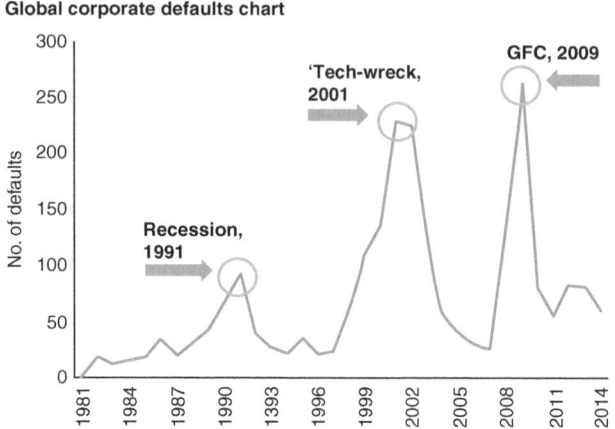

Fig. 2.5 How common are defaults in recent bond investment history?

As noted in Fig. 2.5 there were a total of about 100 defaults by bond issuers in the 1991 recession just after the first Gulf War. About a decade later in 2001 and in the aftermath of the 9/11 terrorist attacks the number of defaults spiked to approximately 230. That figure was eclipsed in 2009 following the Great Financial Crisis with over 250 defaults with many related to sub-prime debt issued in the US housing market sector.

While these figures are sobering, it pays to not be swayed by emotion and look empirically at the facts when assessing the risks associated with bond investing. One should not lose sight of the fact that it is still only a small percentage of the bond issues in the market. As noted in Fig. 2.6, historical data suggests that the chances that your investment in a AAA rated bond with five years until maturity will default is 0.36%. Even if you had the more adventurous appetite of investing in the more risky area of investment grade bonds, let's say a BBB rated bond with five years until maturity, the chances of default would rise to approximately 3%. For the private investor today the percentages show that the chances of a safe outcome in the bond market when you stay within investment grade category are still higher than walking down the street late at night in a major North American city!

Risky forays into the speculative or junk bond world where credit ratings go below BBB, however, show a starker possibility of outcomes with up to 15% chance of default. Private investors seeking the excitement and

Global S&P cumulative default rates (%)

S&P	1 year	2 years	3 years	4 years	5 years
AAA	0.00	0.03	0.14	0.24	0.36
AA+	0.00	0.05	0.05	0.11	0.17
AA	0.02	0.03	0.09	0.23	0.38
AA–	0.03	0.10	0.20	0.28	0.37
A+	0.06	0.11	0.23	0.38	0.51
A	0.07	0.17	0.26	0.40	0.54
A–	0.08	0.20	0.32	0.46	0.66
BBB+	0.13	0.36	0.63	0.91	1.21
BBB	0.19	0.49	0.76	1.18	1.60
BBB–	0.30	0.91	1.63	2.47	(3.29)
Investment grade	0.11	0.29	0.50	0.76	1.03
Speculative grade	3.87	7.58	10.79	13.39	15.49
All rated	1.50	2.95	4.23	5.31	6.20

High grade

Upper medium grade

Lower medium grade

⟵ Lowest investment grade rating

Fig. 2.6 What are the chances of default by credit rating and years until maturity?

high yield of junk bonds should stay within high-yield mutual funds where up to 35–40 bonds might be packaged into a bond fund and exposure to any one bond issue is limited.

As an investment sector, one of the redeeming features of the bond market is its enormous size. The bond markets dwarf all other asset classes. In a 2016 report by fixed income specialist house Nuveen, the size of the global bond market was estimated at USD 87 trillion and slightly double that of the global equity markets at USD 42 trillion. In addition to its size, the bond market has become increasingly international with over 61% of global bond issuers located outside of the United States. While the US Dollar in 2016 still remains the reserve currency of the world used for two thirds of world trade, bonds as a financial instrument have been issued in over 40 countries today and in over 20 different currencies.

Interest Rate Risk

While investing in a bond instrument will give you a fixed return or a set yield until maturity (YTM), bond prices will fluctuate during the life of a bond. If you hold onto a bond until it matures, then your return on the bond will always be equal to the "yield to maturity." However, if you sell a bond before it matures (and many, many investors do), then you are at risk to register a gain or loss depending on how the bond's market price has fluctuated since the date when you bought it.

Bond prices rise when interest rates drop and bond prices fall when interest rates go up. This is very important to remember: There is an inverse relationship between bond prices and interest rates. This means that when medium- or long-term interest rates rise, then bond prices will fall and you may be at risk to lose on your bond investment if you are forced to sell them to gain liquidity.

On the other hand, remember one man's medicine can be another man's poison. While you could lose on a bond investment if you liquidate a position in an interest rate ascending environment, by contrast you could also realize a handsome profit or capital gain if you sold bonds after there was a drop in interest rates owing to government rate cutting actions or other market influences.

How Likely Is a Default in the Global Bond Market?

Rising interest rates are not the only factor that influences bond prices. If a bond issuer, no matter whether it is a government or corporate issuer, undergoes a significant crisis then it could impair its ability to pay its scheduled coupon and it is likely to adversely affect the price of the bond.

Recently this has happened in the case of Greece when government debt in that country began to spiral out of control. As a result the fear of Greek defaulting dramatically impacted the prices of bonds that it had issued in the market. In 2009, Greek government debt yields on ten-year bonds had been priced at a yield of approximately 7% per annum but soared to nearly 35% per annum when the Greek financial crisis fully erupted in 2012–2013. Figured from a price perspective, this might be equivalent to a Greek bond's price falling from about 93 to nearly 65; an investor with USD 100,000 in a Greek bond would have lost over USD 30,000 if forced to sell or too scared to hold on. As noted earlier a notorious private sector default on bonds occurred in 2008 when investment banking giant Lehman Brothers (single A rated at the time) became insolvent and defaulted on bonds it had issued in the market. Many of the bonds had been marketed as mini-bonds to small retail investors in various money market centers. In the Hong Kong market alone, there were over 21,000 lawsuits filed by retail investors seeking to re-claim assets following the Lehman failure.

Defaulting on bond risk has not been the sole domain of private corporations. Argentina, Greece, and Cyprus just to mention a few are sovereign nations who have also defaulted or delayed interest coupon payments to investors in our modern era. In the corporate bond issuer domain the notorious defaults that have occurred within recent history that include the likes of Enron Corporation, an energy sector corporation that defaulted on over USD 13 billion in debt outstanding in 2001 as well as Lehman Brothers, a 150 year old financial institution that had USD 619 billion in debt when it failed in 2008.

Currency devaluation could affect bond pricing, too. If the currency used to issue the bond has depreciated, for example, against the US Dollar, then investors may expect to be compensated in the form of higher bond yields and this could force the price of the bond to fall. In a world where the US Dollar is used to finance almost 65% of world trade, the US Dollar still commands pre-imminent reserve currency status globally. Issuers of debt in non-US Dollar currency often must pay higher yields to investors in order to compensate for the potential currency risk to the investor.

In summary, bonds belong in the portfolio of most investors, especially those who are conservative or moderately aggressive. They represent a promise to repay the investor a fixed return over a defined period of time. Except in periods when the yield curve might be inverted, bond instruments in the three- to ten-year durations usually offer superior yields when compared to time deposits. Compared to the equity asset class which we will cover in later chapters of this book, bond prices tend to be less volatile and represent more stable valuation in the investor's portfolio.

One final note of caution about bonds. At the time of this book going to press, the global economy has gone through an extraordinary bull market period for investors that dates back to the early 1980s when interest rates were an appreciably higher levels and began to fall. Many analysts have been positing views that such a bull market may be coming to any end. Since 2008 the rate of bond issuance globally has mushroomed by 40% and with over one third of the new debt coming from the emerging markets. While such developments are consistent with globalization trends in the world and represent increased opportunities to invest in new areas of the global economy, it also represents a dramatically new set of increased risks. While there are many reputable companies and responsible governments issuing bonds in the market, there are also many bonds being issued in the emerging markets that are relying on financing debt repayment largely from business activity related to commodity export revenues and real estate activity.

Menu du jour: "Ah, some burgers and fries, a shake, and some Junk bonds.....

Fig. 2.7 Riley's Definition of Junk

Another phenomenon emerging most recently in the current global market is the distortion of value being offered for safer bond instruments with higher credit ratings. Investor money chasing higher credit graded bonds have pushed down yields to levels that are even below equity dividend yields. Also accommodative central bank monetary policy and debt restructuring particularly in Europe has resulted yields on up to 40% of outstanding investment grade debt issuance being pushed into negative yield territory. Whereas Japan's central bank policy over the past few decades has ushered into our financial vocabulary the acronym ZIRP (standing for Zero Interest Rate Policy), this new phenomenon has been labeled cynically by critics of the European Central Bank as NIRP (standing for Negative Interest Rate Policy). This is an almost an unprecedented scenario and largely unsustainable. When bond yields are negative in a segment of the bond market there is adequate reason for the investor to avoid exposure until a more normal investment environment returns (Fig. 2.7).

CHAPTER 3

Understanding Equity Markets

Did You Know?

It is believed that the first modern stock markets began in modern-day Belgium in the city of Antwerp around 1409 in a building owned by a merchant family named Van der Beurze. The building was used as meeting place where local merchants could exchange debt notes. Soon after "Beurzen" meetings began to occur in nearby cities. It is believed the world "bourse" (commonly used in English and French to describe a stock exchange) may have evolved from this family name.

If you want to achieve superior investment returns, you will need to have equity exposure in your investment portfolio. Plainly said, holding ownership in shares or equities in a company is tantamount to having fractional ownership in the company in proportion to the total number of shares outstanding. The shareholder is "last man standing" after all claims such as debt (bondholders) are discharged when a company fails or "files for Chapter 11." Thus, shareholders have the most to lose in event of a company default. However, compared to bondholders who only receive a fixed interest from debt holdings in a company, shareholders in a company potentially have the most to gain if a company prospers.

Here are some key points to remember about investing in equity products.

© The Author(s) 2017
B. VonCannon, *A Guidebook for Today's Asian Investor*,
https://doi.org/10.1007/978-981-10-5831-8_3

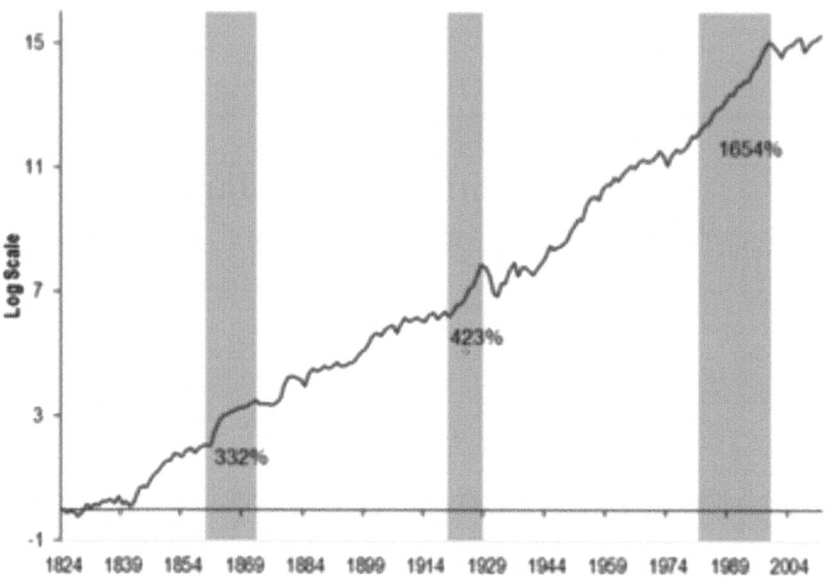

Fig. 3.1 Why Time Horizon is Important! A sampling of US equity prices since early 1900s as seen through US large company stock total returns. Note: This chart emphasizes the importance of being patient and having a long time horizon when investing in the equity markets. Over time equities outperform all the other asset classes! Source: BofA Merrill Lynch Global Investment Strategy, Ibbotson

TIME HORIZON

Have a suitable time horizon for equity investments.

In general, you should be very, very careful investing in the equity markets if you do not have a multi-year investment time horizon. Equity investing is most suitable to a three- to five-year time horizon. In any one year, equity investments may underperform (actually performing worse than time deposits or bonds!). However, over a multi-year time horizon, equities normally outperform time deposits and bonds.

DIVERSIFICATION USUALLY WORKS IN YOUR FAVOR WHEN SELECTING EQUITIES FOR YOUR INVESTMENT PORTFOLIO

Equities can be dissected and categorized across several asset classes. They are normally dissected according to industry. Here would be some typical industry categories.

Consumer discretionary: stocks that deal with products or services that are not necessities (e.g. automobiles, high-end clothing, restaurants, hotel groups, and luxury goods).

Consumer non-discretionary: stocks that deal with products or services that are non-cyclical meaning they are always in demand no matter how well the economy is performing. People tend to consume the products of these companies at a relatively constant level regardless of price (e.g. companies selling products like toiletries, tobacco, cleaning and paper products).

Utilities: stocks of companies that provide a set of services often state owned but also sometimes privately held that provide electricity, natural gas, water, sewage, and telephone services.

Technology: stocks relating to research, development, and distribution of technology-based goods and services.

Internet of things (IOT): stocks providing network of physical objects or "things" embedded with electronics, software, sensors, and connecting to enable objects to exchange data.

Healthcare: a category of stocks relating to medical and healthcare goods and services.

Banking, finance, and insurance: stocks from companies that provide a range of financial products and services.

Natural resources: a category of stocks related to oil, coal, natural gas, water, and mineral ores such as copper, aluminum, gold, and silver.

Equities can also be dissected and categorized across company size. Here would be some ways to categorize in this manner.

Large cap: stocks of companies with market capital of more than USD 10 billion.

Small and medium (SME) size cap: stocks of small- and medium-sized enterprises which mostly have market cap under USD 10 billion.

Growth stocks: stocks which mainly offer attractiveness to the investor through stock price appreciation (rather than dividend payout) and often associated with the term "growth investing" vs. "value investing."

Value stocks: stocks normally associated with companies that trade at a discount to book value, have high dividend payouts, and/or have low P/E ratios or price-to-book ratios.

High dividend yield stocks: stocks whose dividend yield is higher than the yield of any benchmark average such as the ten-year US Treasury Note.

There could also be an argument for looking at diversification in the stock market on a geographical or country-by-country basis. Currently there are 60 major global stock market indexes in the world today comprising approximately 50 trillion dollars. If we examine the global equity markets on a capitalization basis, currently North American stock markets comprise 40% of total global equity market cap, followed by Asia totaling 33% of global market cap led by Japan and China, and then Europe with approximately 19%. The current predominance of the North American stock market in some respects reflects the strong tradition of corporate governance, variety of selection, and the vast daily trading volume and liquidity of the US market. Whether or not the investor should invest a significant portion of his assets in the US market or other global equity markets, or one's home equity market becomes an issue for the investor that reflects his or her base currency and risk tolerance and desire for portfolio diversification. This subject will be discussed in further detail in Chapter 7.

Price Volatility

If you cannot take price volatility, you probably should not invest in equities. Just remember this is why you need to have a longer time horizon when you invest in equities.

Avoid trying to be a "market timer." You will never guess perfectly the bottom of a market. You will never guess the perfect time to sell either.

It may be useful to extol the virtues of patience and calm during periods of equity market volatility. If one can avoid panic response, it might be useful to examine past historical patterns in equity markets. Figure this, there have been 11 bear markets in the S & P 500 since 1929. The shortest bear market lasted three months (1990) and the longest of these bear markets, occurring just after World War II, lasted about three years, 1946–1949. While almost all of these bear market periods were multi-year, the average duration was about 16 months. What is more important to remember is that the rebounds from bear markets tend to be quite robust. In all of these 11 examples, the average recovery one year after the trough in the bear market was in excess of 25%. In fact, in almost half the cases, the rebounds in the equity market were over 40%. In these 11 examples equity market returns five years after the start of the recovery were up 80% to 200%.

Looking historically at the upswings in the market also underscores the importance of patience and adopting a suitable time horizon. Until our most recent equity bull market run there had been 11 great bull market runs in the S & P 500 since the Great Depression. Judging from these 11 buoyant market runs we can see that the average bull market upswing typically lasts 58 months (i.e. almost five years) and the cumulative return during such time period averages 167%. A more recent example may be even more pertinent. The recent S & P 500 bull market which began following the financial crisis in 2008 had already surpassed 90 months in duration by the beginning of 2017. Its return had been over 200% through the first quarter of 2017 and thereby exceeding the average return of almost all of the previous ten other bull markets.

When equity market prices are volatile and the stock indices show no smooth sailing in sight one may be tempted to flee exposure to the market. However, history favors the investor maintaining exposure to the equity markets even when there are systemic corrections. Just remember every downturn in the New York Stock Exchange since its founding in 1790 has resulted in the market rising again to reach new heights. When one invests in equities there will be bumps in the road! Maintaining a sense of optimism in view of these periods of volatility is important and history has proven time and time again this to be the case.

	Price Change	Dividend Dist. Rate	Total Return	Inflation	Real Price Change	Real Total Return
1950's	13.2 %	5.4 %	19.3 %	2.2 %	10.7 %	16.7 %
1960's	4.4 %	3.3 %	7.8 %	2.5 %	1.8 %	5.2 %
1970's	1.6 %	4.3 %	5.8 %	7.4 %	−5.4 %	−1.4 %
1980's	12.6 %	4.6 %	17.3 %	5.1 %	7.1 %	11.6 %
1990's	15.3 %	2.7 %	18.1 %	2.9 %	12.0 %	14.7 %
2000's	−2.7 %	1.8 %	−1.0 %	2.5 %	−5.1 %	−3.4 %
1950–2009	7.2 %	3.6 %	11.0 %	3.8 %	3.3 %	7.0 %

Fig. 3.2 Over time statistics favor staying in the market! Source: www.simple-stockinvesting.com. Simple Stock Investing (using S & P 500 returns and U.S. BOL CPI figures)

Annual Returns of the S & P Index- Positive years vs. Negative years

Return variances in percentage ranges

50% to 60%	'33 '54				
40% to 50%	'28 35 '58				
30% to 40%	'27 '36 '38	'45 '50 '55	'75 '80 '85	'85 '89 '91	'95 '97 '13
20% to 30%	'42 '43 '51	'61 '63 '67	'76 '82 '83	'90 '98 '99	'03 '09
10% to 20%	'26 '44 '49	'52 '59 '64	'65 '68 '71	'72 '79 '86	'88 '93 '04 '06 '10 '12 '14
0% to 10%	'47 '48 '56	'60 '70 '78	'84 '87 '92	'94 '05 '07	'11

65 plus years

0% to -10%	'29 '32 '34	'39 '40 '46	'53 '62 '69	'77 '81 '90	'00
-10 to'-20%	'41 '57 '66	'73 '01			
-20 to'-30%	'30 '74 '02				
-30 to'-40%	'37 '08				**24 minus years**
-40 to'-50%	'31				

---

10 Year Market returns of S&P 500 index- Positive vs. Negative
10 Year periods ending in these years!

'35 '36 '37	'40 '41 '42	'43 '44 '45	'46 '47
'48 '49 '50	'51 '52 '53	'54 '55 '56	'57 '58
'59 '60 '61	'62 '63 '64	'65 '66 '67	'68 '69
'70 '71 '72	'73 '74 '75	'76 '77 '78	'79 '80
'81 '82 '83	'84 '85 '86	'87 '88 '89	'90 '91
'92 '93 '94	'95 '96 '97	'98 '99 '00	'01 '02
'03 '04 '05	'06 '07 '10	'11 '12 '13	'14

76 plus 10 year periods

'38 '39 '08	'09		

4 minus 10 year periods

Fig. 3.3 History Favors a Return to the Mean! Source: Morningstar, Franklin Templeton

CHAPTER 4

Derivatives and Structured Products

> **Did You Know?**
> The earliest known use of the financial option dates to second century BC Greece when green olive farmers during times of bumper harvests purportedly began to pay advances to reserve use of olive presses for making olive oil. Today use of options is widely conducted in foreign exchange, equity, fixed income, and other areas of finance. The Chicago Board of Options Exchange (BOE) was established in 1973 setting up an institution that guarantees standardized derivative transactions.

In addition to gaining an understanding about the three major asset classes discussed in the previous chapters, it is important to grasp an understanding of some of the new types of products that have been introduced and spread rapidly in the market in recent years. Some of these products and the terms affiliated with their daily usage may seem intimidating. However, don't be cowed! Learn to use these products to your advantage and you will have better investment results.

Let's start first by describing what we mean when we use the word derivative in the financial world. A derivative can be defined as a contract between two or more parties whose value is based on an agreed upon underlying asset, like a stock, a bond, a commodity, interest rates, market indexes, or units of a currency. Specifically such contracts are normally associated with using financial products that can include futures contracts,

© The Author(s) 2017
B. VonCannon, *A Guidebook for Today's Asian Investor*,
https://doi.org/10.1007/978-981-10-5831-8_4

forward contracts, options, swaps, and warrants. Such instruments usually create a contract between two parties whose value is based upon an agreed upon price at some future date.

Certain types of derivatives, let's say in the case of commodity derivatives, can mitigate risk and really almost be considered like "insurance" to the writer of the option or contract holder. Used in a more aggressive manner, derivatives are sometimes used by speculators seeking to make a profit in times of market volatility. Many derivatives are traded as "over the counter" instruments, meaning they are negotiated in person, by phone, or electronic contact between two parties. In addition, there are over 30 national exchanges in countries around the world that conduct derivatives trading. An exchange-traded derivative contract that exists from an underlying asset that is listed on a trading exchange is guaranteed against default through a clearinghouse. It is for this reason that exchange traded derivatives normally have a higher degree of liquidity and trade more easily on the secondary market.

The widespread use of derivatives over the past 20 years has spawned a new category of products called "structured products." In many situations the minimum amount of investment capital needing to be put at risk in order to set up a derivative position may constitute too great of a percentage of the investor's portfolio to justify a single derivative position. For example, currency options are often marketed to investors in face amounts of USD 500,000 to 1 million and are initiated by the investor paying a premium that might be up to 2% or more of the face value of the option position. One way in which investors have been able to attain some derivative exposure and risk smaller amounts of their investment capital is via the method of investing in a structured product.

The proliferation of structured products as a component of investment portfolios has become more and more common particularly since the mid-1990s when derivative products mostly in the form of options started to become accessible to the normal investor. Structured products are essentially packaged investment products with derivative products embedded into the product with the intention of achieving a particular investment enhancement with a defined investment period. With technology entering into the workplace steadily since the 1990s, the use of structured products has expanded exponentially. It is as if there has been a steroid shot being made available to investors in the financial markets.

The use of derivative technology in managing mutual funds has also spawned the rapid expansion of a class of alternative funds (often called "hedge funds"). Such funds are sometimes referred to as the fourth major asset class after money market, fixed income, and equity asset classes. Alternative funds are different from traditional mutual funds. Traditional mutual funds are funds that normally hold exposure to a selection of 20 or 30 to bonds or stocks names that offer investment reward when the asset prices in the mutual fund increase in value. In the alternative fund world the fund manager often uses derivative strategies that can produce positive returns even when the bond or equity market falls in value. The alternative fund manager may adopt a "market neutral strategy" which may reward the investor even when the bond market or equity market falls. For example, an alternative equity fund manager may believe that the market price of a certain stock may fall in value in the coming year. As a result he may buy a put option on a certain stock name or sell a call option which, if he is correct in his prediction, would reward the fund performance if the strike price of the option of this stock remained "in the money" at the expiry of the option period. Alternative fund managers pride themselves on being able to deliver positive investment performance that has low correlation with the performance of the stock market.

In some corners of the financial news media it has become fashionable in recent years to vilify the use of structured products and hedge funds. This is largely due to a misunderstanding over how such products were originally intended to be used. No doubt some excesses have occurred in recent years in regard to the use of derivatives and mostly by a minority of the people working in the financial community. The vast majority of wealth managers and private bankers have used structured products and alternative funds as tools for controlling or limiting risk (not increasing client risk!) and with the best interests of the investor at heart.

Here is how structured products can help you.

First, in situations in which it is needed, they mitigate against the risk of having long exposure in the market. Using this term "long exposure" is another way of saying one is holding the asset. The problem with investing only in the three major asset classes (cash deposits, bonds, and equities) is that you will go through periods when the market is very volatile and your portfolio value may have significant swings in value.

Since the mid-1990s options have become much more a part of daily investing. While some journalists or critics of the financial industry like to paint options as dangerous, risky products, the real truth is that options were invented to help investors reduce risk. If used in the proper manner, they can help investors do just that—reduce volatility and uncertainty in returns.

Let's discuss some of the ways you can use options to improve your financial performance.

Fig. 4.1   *"Did you say he is the new guy on the structured products desk?"* Note: This figure is intended to be a pun on the view of structured products in the financial markets today. Often such products have derivatives imbedded in them and have been compared to putting steroids into investing—can generate great returns but one must beware of potential side effects (i.e. risks)

USING OPTIONS IN THE MONEY MARKET SEGMENT OF YOUR INVESTMENT PORTFOLIO

Currency options are a popular tool used by international investors who are active in the global currency markets. Take for example if you were a US Dollar based currency investor, you might only be receiving a modest monthly return from placing funds in US Dollar time deposits. At current rates, it might be less than 1% per annum.

However, if you were willing to risk putting a little bit of your deposit money into another currency (like Euro, British pounds, Yen, or Gold) then you could roll over a series of time deposits and possibly earn up to 5% or 6% per annum on the cash invested.

Structured Product # 1: The Dual Currency Deposit

One of the most popular products for investors in Asia over the past two decades has been a short-term, relatively low risk product that enhances time deposit returns in one currency while putting the investor at risk to receiving a return in another currency. It has been especially popular in the near zero interest rate environment in which we have been living in the past 15 years.

The product is commonly called by the name "Dual Currency Deposit" at several financial institutions or may be also referred to in banker logo as a "DCD" or "DCI." The Swiss tend to call it by slightly different name, "DOCU."

Let's suppose that US Dollar time deposit rates at the financial institution where you keep your investment account are currently being quoted at 2% per annum for a 1 month time deposit and you are thinking of placing USD 200,000 into a time deposit for one month. Let's suppose that the US Dollar/ Euro FX rate is being quoted spot at 1.0715 after the Euro has weakened in recent weeks from 1.11 to the current 1.0715 level. If you think Euro might stabilize for a foreseeable time at this 1.07 level then it might be a suitable time for you to place your USD 200,000 into a one month DCD and seek a rate that is higher than the current unattractive time deposit rate.

After calling your private banker you are offered a quote for a 30 day time deposit at 6.0% per annum (rather than the abysmal 2% rate for a plain vanilla time deposit rate). If you will accept a strike price of 1.0574---------------meaning that as long as the US Dollar/ Euro FX rate remains above the 1.0574 level at the expiration one month later, then you will receive back your principal, USD 200,000, plus interest of 6.0% annualized. This would be called a DCD that has "lapsed" or expired "in the money." If, however, the Euro currency continued during the coming days to depreciate below the current spot level of 1.0715 and 1 month later was below 1.0574 at, let's say, 1.0550 or 1.0375, then you would receive back your principal and interest in Euro currency and the conversion rate would be at the strike price (1.0574). In this latter case the investor is "out of the money" and will be "exercised" into the alternative currency.

Under this structured product scenario, if the Euro has depreciated too dramatically upon expiry at the end of 30 days, then you would stand to lose the advantage of the higher interest rate quoted in the DCD. The higher the interest rate differential would be wiped out by FX loss. However, if during the one month period the Euro stabilizes at the 1.07 level or only slightly lower, then you would receive back your principal and interest in U.S. Dollars at the expiration of the DCD.

The beauty of DCD products is that they often can be quoted in many types of combinations of currencies or precious metals (like gold and silver) and for various tenors as short as a few days to 6 months or longer. In Asia, many investors like DCDs in combinations like USD/Euro, USD/Yen, and USD/Gold and tenors like two weeks or 1 month tend to be the most common time lengths. They can even be set in combinations using Euro as the base currency and with a play on the other currencies like Euro/ Yen, Euro/ Sterling, or Euro/ Gold. The DCD product can also be broken down by the private banker and sold in smaller denominations to investors (usually minimum of USD

125,000) than if the investor himself wanted to buy a call or put option outright.

The financial institutions are able to offer such product because there is adequate liquidity that allows for a derivatives market. If trading volume is low and there is little or no volatility, then conditions for setting call options and put options on currencies is less ideal. It is the large volume of foreign exchange trading daily globally which creates a highly liquid market that makes settling such products easy. The volume of foreign exchange trading markets daily are perhaps the largest and most liquid markets in the world. While daily trading volume has been slipping slightly the past three years after hitting a peak of approximately USD 6 trillion per day in 2014, it is still substantial at over USD 4.5 trillion per day. In currencies that are not freely traded or have extremely low levels of liquidity, an FX options market would likely not exist and the DCD structured product would not be possible.

The example cited above most likely involved the private banker using the underlying USD 200,000 deposit in combination with a put option embedded into the DCD product quote with a strike at 1.0574. When writing (or selling) a put, the investor receives a premium that can be added to the time deposit interest amount and it is that premium amount which allows the private banker to set the DCD interest level to be set at the higher 6.0% per annum level compared to the plain vanilla time deposit rate of 2.0% per annum. If the investor's strike price (1.0574) is breached upon expiry of the deposit, then the U.S. Dollars are "put" to the option buyer. That is why the investor will receive principal and interest in a different (i.e. the Euro) currency.

Now, don't get me wrong. You would be exposed to some currency risk. However, if you managed the selection and timing well, you could vastly improve the return on the cash deposit segment of your portfolio.

Here is how a dual currency deposit (DCD) works.

Let's suppose you are frustrated with the fact that your bank certificates of deposit (CDs) or time deposits in US Dollar denomination for one-month tenor are being quoted at a rate under 1% per annum.

You follow the foreign exchange markets a bit and see that the US Dollar has strengthened dramatically against other currencies or that Gold has fallen below its 270-day moving average. This might be a good time to explore booking a DCD for let's say one month. You will need to set a strike price with your private banker. Bear in mind you will be at risk to being struck or converted into the alternative currency or metal on the expiry date if the strike price has been breached.

Let's also suppose that you are not worried about the risk of being converted into Gold or another currency like Euro or Yen. (By the way, I remember a client that used to import manufacturing machinery from Germany and Japan and did not worry about being converted into either currency.) If you have access to international investing, you can ask your private banker to quote a 30- or 60-day DCD rate at an agreed upon interest rate of, let's say, 6% per annum.

USING OPTIONS WITH THE BOND OR FIXED INCOME PORTION OF YOUR PORTFOLIO

A popular investment scheme in the first decade of the new millennium after 2000 involving fixed income products was something called CDRAN (sort of like saying "See how Douglas ran," it was labeled "See D ran!).

A typical CDRAN might offer the investor a set deposit rate for a fore-seeable future. For example, many CDRANs in the early days offered clients rates like 7% per annum in return for certain market conditions remaining in place. Here is one of my favorites.

Year Guaranteed Note
Rate: 7% per annum
Callable: Quarterly
Terms and Conditions: The three-month US Dollar LIBOR rate must remain above 4% p.a.

Structured Product Example: #2; The Callable Range Accrual Note

Another very popular structured product that existed in the international wealth management market a few years ago was the so-call CDRAN (pronounced like "C DEE RAN!). Technically it stood for "Callable Range Accrual Note." Practically speaking it was both a very valuable way for investors to earn a premium in short term debt paper and all the while only taking on a calculable and what many would consider low risk. The clients loved it; the banks made a fortune offering it.

CDRAN products were issued by private banks in those days who were packaging debt issued by U.S. government agencies like Fannie Mae and Freddy Mac who, in turn, were financing debt obligations coming largely from the large mass of home buyers across the United States. The fact that it was a U.S. government agency issuing the notes implied that the notes offered were guaranteed by the U.S. government and merited AAA credit rating status. The real truth was that they were NOT in fact guaranteed by the U.S. government and nor were they really genuine AAA rated debt notes. However, the aura of being a U.S. government agency made investors feel safe.

At the time the typical U.S. dollar one month and three month time deposit rates were only offering yields in the 4% per annum range. However, the CDRAN product was a value proposition that went like this. We will pay you 7% per annum for a 1 or 2 year debt obligation. Investors were more than happy to lock in the rate for a short tenor at a rate that was at least 3% higher than normal time deposit rate. Think about it. For every USD 1 million purchased, a 3% interest rate differential means you can earn an extra USD 30,000 per year. Furthermore, most wealth management banks offering the CDRAN product, in fact, offered credit lines against 80% of the value of the note which was a further sign that it was safe to invest in.

In the issuing memorandum for each of these notes it typically mentioned that these notes were callable quarterly if the US Dollar Libor 3 month rate were to go below a certain level, let's say 4%. What it meant practically was that many of these notes were called after 3 months or 6 months as short term US Dollar rates in the years following 9/11 were low and often falling. The term "calling" a note means that the issuer has the right to give the investor back his principal and accrued interest a specified time intervals described in the note memorandum. However, the issuers of such debt notes were more than happy to re-issue new notes in the market at slightly lower rates but still with very attractive yields vis-a-vis time deposit rates.

The story of CDRAN notes similar to the one described above did not die a sudden death. They sort of faded out of vogue after the sub-prime crisis in 2008 as short term interest rates and LIBOR fell to unprecedented lows— — — —-what we call the zero interest rate environment. Also the shaky credit standing that Fannie Mae and Freddie Mac suffered subsequent to 2008 made investors more wary of investing into CDRAN type products with such underlying debt obligations.

USING OPTIONS WITH THE EQUITY PORTION OF YOUR PORTFOLIO

A popular investment scheme involving use of an option might look something like this equity linked note product called a "PERLE."

Your private banker offers you a selection of stocks which you like and notes that because they are traded in fairly high daily volumes it provides

Structured Product Example #3- The Equity Linked Note

An Equity Linked note (or "ELN" as it is called within the ranks of private bankers) can be structured for the investor in order to make advantage of some foreseen movement in the price of the equity or basket of equities. One very popular type of ELN would be one that offers the investor a fixed return that is in excess of the short term deposit rates. The guaranteed enhanced return is achieved by combining a time deposit with a derivative that has a stock share as the underlying asset.

In the example below, a client likes the stock share DBS Bank that is selling at a price of 10.30 per share on the Singapore Stock Exchange. The investor checks his local private banker and informs him that he is interested to invest SGD 200,000. The investor further learns that the consensus of analysts in the market believe the share price may not continue to rise in value in the coming months. However, they also believe the share will have a stable price range in the coming months.

So the investor checks ELN opportunities with the private banker who quote him a return of 9.5% per annum on the share for the coming 3 months with a strike at 10% below the current share price of 10.30 per share. The quote is a good return when compared to the time deposit rates in Singapore dollar which are 2% per annum. This means he can achieve 7.5% interest rate differential by investing in the ELN rather than a plain vanilla time deposit. The only caveat is that if in 90 days upon expiry of the ELN, if the share price has fallen more than 10% below the current share price (that is below 9.27 per share), then the investor will receive back the share issued at strike price rather than the cash he put up for the 3 month investment tenor.

ELNs are popular with investors because they are relatively easy to put together into a structured product so long as the underlying share has adequate daily trading liquidity in the market. Stock shares will low trading volume would not be eligible for structuring ELNs. The ELN can also be broken down and offered in relatively small amounts compared to buying or selling an option outright. Even in cases when an investor is occasionally struck and exercised into the share at the end of the investment tenor, the share will usually go up in value over time.

enough liquidity for him to offer you an equity linked note. Let's say that you particularly like a stock named "DBS Bank" and it has been range trading the past half year at 10.30 per share. Your private banker then says I will offer you a flat guarantee rate of 8% per annum for the next 90 days as long as DBS Bank stock price is at least above 9.27 per share. If the stock price is below 9.27 at the end of 90 days, rather than receive back your cash, you must take the share at the strike price of 9.27 per share.

If you like DBS Bank you might think that in return for 8% p.a., it is a safe bet. There are two scenarios under which you might decide not to invest in the PERLE. One, if you felt nervous and did not like the stock fearing it might plummet into the $8.00 range, then you might not invest in the PERLE. Or, if you really liked DBS and thought the price might go to $11 or $12 per share, then you would be better off just buying the share as such price increase would offer a potential return well above the 8% p.a. offered by the PERLE.

In summary, use of derivative strategies involves delicate pricing and timing when placing a structured product into an investment portfolio. When choosing alternative fund exposure for the portfolio, selecting more than one type of alternative fund is often a wise strategy. Reckless entrees by the investor into the derivative markets without well-conceived tactical consideration can be extremely risky and easily become destructive to one's wealth rather than preserving it. Working with a competent wealth manager or financial broker is essential in order to pair the proper derivative exposure with your portfolio.

Volumes of books have been written on derivative products and strategies for using them. It would be impossible to cover every facet of derivative strategy in this one chapter. Computer technology and statistical analysis programs have been applied to the pricing of derivative products on trading desks for many years and incorporate sophisticated computer modules like Black-Scholes and Value at Risk (VaR). It is not necessary to memorize these theories in order to use derivative instruments to your advantage. The key thing is merely to understand in broad terms how they work to grow your wealth and mitigate against risk.

For the majority of investors it is wiser to use structured products and alternative funds as a means for having derivative exposure and for the purposes of hedging risk rather than investing directly into the naked derivative instrument. While there is often a profit built into structured products for the bank or broker that offers them, it is often worth the protection and safety that such products can offer. This can be accomplished easily by coordinating with a wealth management specialist or financial broker. Investors commonly use derivative exposure for the purpose of hedging currency positions, hedging against changes in interest rates, or protecting one's positions in the equity markets. That being said, no doubt you will encounter speculators looking for a quick profit, and who are often assuming very high risk derivative strategies involving leverage. There is a large graveyard of failed structured product strategies and poorly used derivative strategies. There are even some well-constructed, structured products that just did not work out because market conditions changed abruptly. One should be disciplined in one's approach to investing in structured products and diversify one's exposure over more than one type of product idea. Winning in investing is a bit like analyzing a baseball player's batting average. No baseball player ever batted 1000 and no investor ever has ever been successful 100% of the time. Being successful in most (not all) of your structured product and alternative fund selections will make you a successful investor in the long run.

CHAPTER 5

The Key to Investing Wisely

Did You Know?
A recent study by S & P Dow Jones Indices on the performance after fees of 25,000 actively managed mutual funds over the past decade showed that over 86% of them failed to outperform their benchmark. Such a report is consistent with the growing trend in recent years of investors selecting index tracker exchange traded funds (ETFs) over actively managed mutual funds.

Over the years I must confess that I picked up some valuable principles from some of the wiser persons that I worked with. I cannot emphasize enough the importance of having a framework or vision in your mind of how you want to structure the portfolio. The following four principles may help you set up that framework. They are some of the most valuable bits of advice handed down to me and I will share with you. It goes like this: If you invest, have a very clear picture in your mind of the following.

HAVE A TIME HORIZON

A time horizon is key to your being able to pick a winning investment strategy. Once you have selected the proper mix of assets for your portfolio, remain committed to it. This does not mean that you will not make some adjustments or rotate some selections in or out of the portfolio.

© The Author(s) 2017
B. VonCannon, *A Guidebook for Today's Asian Investor*,
https://doi.org/10.1007/978-981-10-5831-8_5

However, never forget that lot of investment products are best suited to a specifically set time horizon.

For example, if your time horizon is limited to only one year, be very careful investing in bonds and equities. Why? It is because they are most suitable for time horizons which are longer than one year. They are best suited for three- to five-year time horizons. It does not mean that you will not adjust your positions as you go along. Quite the contrary! Always check, always review. However, do not panic in the face of market volatility.

Set Your Own Internal Risk Tolerance Level

From earlier discussion in this book you will have learned a little bit about risk that is inherent in the major asset classes (cash deposits, bonds/fixed income, and equities).

One tactic which might be helpful to you is to check the price variability of a specific asset or group of assets. Most databases (e.g. Reuters,

This is a can't miss you know, everyone likes horses right!

Fig. 5.1   Set your own Internal Risk Tolerance Level

Bloomberg, and Telekurs) will be able to help you locate the pricing history of the asset that you are reviewing. In the world of equities, the historical standard deviation of a stock price's annual return measured against its performance is called the "Sharpe Ratio." It is literally measured as follows:

$$\text{Sharpe Ratio} = \frac{(AR - RF)}{Pr}$$

AR = Annual Return of a stock, RF = *Risk Free Rate, Pr = The Standard deviation of the stock price. * The risk free rate is the theoretical return of an investment with no risk of financial loss. Most academicians would consider the US Dollar 90-day Treasury bill rate to be a suitable "risk free rate" proxy because there is no credit risk and the maturity is so short that is little or no market risk.

Some stocks will provide you with good annual returns but will give you ulcers with their price fluctuation. This comes out in the wash when you compare Sharpe Ratios.

HAVE A RETURN EXPECTATION

It is important to know that all investment choices have risk.

Some people think if they put all their money in cash, then they will not lose and will maintain their level of wealth. Nothing could be further from the truth. In addition to the risk of the institution where you deposit your cash, a key risk of keeping your wealth denominated totally in cash is that it will not keep track with the rate of inflation.

Over time inflation erodes the value of any cash currency. That is why the price of goods and services (e.g. your grocery bill or your dental bill) goes up over time. If inflation averages a 3% annual rate over a five-year time period and your money is left entirely in cash, then over that period of time, the buying power of your cash will fall by approximately 15%. Clearly if someone said to you I am going to take 15% of your cash out of your pocket, then you would be phoning the local sheriff, right? That is what happens to the value of holding cash over long time periods if not invested. It loses its purchasing value. It is a dent in your net worth!

So stay alert to the false illusion that by holding cash you are preserving wealth when you maybe doing just the opposite. Place a value or price on holding cash just like you would if you were holding a property or another asset in your investment portfolio.

Another useful perspective to adopt as you reflect on your net worth and how you invest it each year is to start thinking in terms of "real return." Here is the meaning of "real return:"

$$Real\ Return = Nominal\ Return - Inflation\ Rate$$

If you have a cash deposit that is earning a nominal return of 1% per annum and the annual inflation rate is 3%, then your real return is –2%. In other words, the value of your wealth is falling by 2% yearly.

On the other hand, if you can achieve a nominal 5% annual return when the inflation rate is 3%, then your wealth is increasing as your real return is a positive 2%.

Did you know that if you could achieve a positive 4% annual real return that your net worth would double over a period of 18 years?

Also take note, if your real return is only a positive 1%, it will take 72 years for your net worth to double in value.

Have a Yardstick for Managing Investment Success

As confusing as the investment world can be, one useful way of making sense of the proper path for yourself is to establish a sort of benchmark to your investing. Benchmarks allow us to measure performance relative to a set or assumed group of risk parameters. One cannot properly measure the successfulness of a return without assessing the risks that were endured when the investment was made.

One benchmark that is key for international investors is that of adopting a "base currency" or "reference currency." Base currency is a sort of yard-stick for determining the annual return or value of appreciation or deterioration in an investment portfolio. For example, the typical international investor may invest in assets denominated in more than one currency. However, at the end of each year the investor will use one of the currencies to measure the performance of the investment portfolio. That currency is considered the "base currency."

Currently most investors from North America and even many countries in Latin America and Asia use the US Dollar as their "base currency." It is normally their choice of "base currency" because their domestic currencies are pegged or under "managed float" with the value of the US Dollar. This is especially true in Asia where the Hong Kong Dollar, the New

Fig. 5.2

Taiwan Dollar, the Chinese Renminbi, the Singapore Dollar, and Thai Baht are all closely linked to the US Dollar. There are also exceptions in Asia! For example, most Australians choose the Australian Dollar as their base currency and most Japanese consider the Yen as their base currency.

In countries across the European continent, it is most likely the case that the Euro or Swiss Franc would be considered to be the typical investor's "base currency." In the UK, one would likely find residents there selecting the British Pound (Sterling) to be the base currency.

Rule of thumb is one should maintain one's portfolio between 40% and 60% in one's base currency at all times. However, in recent years in which we have seen dramatic swings in foreign exchange rates exceeding 10–20% in one year, there has been a trend to be even more conservative with regard to managing one's foreign exchange exposure. It has not been uncommon to find investors keeping 80% of their portfolios denominated in the base currency.

One additional general comment on currencies is that US Dollar remains the most widely used currency in the world today and maintains the role as "reserve currency" for most of the world. It is estimated by various analysts that about two thirds of global trade is denominated in US Dollar.

The US Dollar replaced the British Pound as global reserve currency after the Bretton Woods Conference in 1944 following years of economic decline in the British Empire that began after World War I.

The other major global currencies of the world used for international trade are the Euro, Japanese Yen, British Sterling (or Pound), and (since October 2016) the Chinese Renminbi (RMB). In this regard the International Monetary Fund (IMF) has granted these currencies Special Drawing Rights (SDR). As we enter the second decade of the twenty-first century, consistent with China's rising global economic status is the decision by the IMF that the Chinese currency, RMB, will assume a more global status in the years to come. The RMB was once a closed currency to the outside world, but in 2016 the IMF approved China's application to make the RMB an SDR currency. The RMB is still not used in more than 10% of international trade transactions and it is unlikely to replace the US Dollar as global reserve currency overnight! However, the trend is clear. The RMB is becoming increasingly more recognized in world trade and investment activity.

Another technique to include in assessing portfolio or an asset's performance is to compare one's investment to a known "benchmark." Among the most common benchmarks used in comparing equity performance is the Morgan Stanley Composite Index (MSCI). Other ones commonly used might include the Financial Times Stock Exchange (FTSE) 100 and the EURO STOXX 50.

Don't Put All Your Eggs in One Basket

A gentleman named Dr. Harry Markowitz won the Nobel Prize in Finance in 1990 for his theory on how to allocate assets. His original book, produced in 1952, was called "Portfolio Selection." As readers and followers studied his writings, they began to refer to Markowitz's theories under the theme of "Modern Portfolio Theory."

Markowitz was seeking to extol the advantages of "efficient portfolio diversification." He believed very strongly and, in fact, backed up his theory with data that suggested that the wise investor over time could achieve the best possible investment return outcome by diversifying his asset selection into several asset classes.

Another way of saying this is, "Don't put all your eggs into one basket."

If you will recall the key features of the major asset classes (cash deposits, bonds and fixed income, equities, and alternative investments), keep in mind that not one of these asset classes will perform best every year. Over a period of ten years it has been proven that equities outperform the other asset classes. Alternative investments as a separate sort of hybrid asset class in many recent analytical studies are a close second place. Bonds or fixed income instruments in any ten-year time period will also likely have one or two years when they achieve a better return than equities. Cash deposits, the most conservative of the asset classes, will rarely give the best annual return and only seldom outperform the other asset classes.

Fig. 5.3

CHAPTER 6

Three Useful Concepts to Investing Wisely

Did You Know?
The earliest writings on statistical analysis and numerical frequency can be traced to fourteenth century Islamic philosopher, Al-Kindi. He is reputed to have written over 260 books during his lifetime which also covered topics including medicine, physics, and philosophy. Many of his books have been lost over time. An important discovery in a library in Turkey in the twentieth century has preserved some of his valuable contributions.

There are many things that affect the financial markets and there are many theories and concepts about its behavior.

Over the years I have found three concepts helpful in bettering one's understanding of how the markets behave.

Understanding Systemic Risk vs. Non-systemic Risk

One major concept that I think is critical to understand is that of systemic risk. Systemic risk is the risk of collapse of an entire financial system or entire market as opposed to "non-systemic risk" which normally pertains to one stock or specific group of stocks.

© The Author(s) 2017
B. VonCannon, *A Guidebook for Today's Asian Investor*,
https://doi.org/10.1007/978-981-10-5831-8_6

When there is systemic risk in the market, virtually everything is prone to price decline or reduction in asset value. When systemic risk hits the stock market, then virtually every stock will be impacted.

Some notorious examples of systemic corrections in the financial markets would be the Great Depression in 1929 or the sub-prime crisis in 2008 which fostered a steep decline in the market.

Let's compare systemic risk to its antithesis which is called "non-systemic risk." Non-systemic risk by definition is the risk associated with holding any individual stock.

What is important to remember is when there is systemic risk, the price of almost everything will be affected. Conversely, according to modern portfolio theory, non-systemic risk in an investment portfolio can be contained by investing in stocks that have low or inverse correlation with each other.

THE CONCEPT OF CORRELATION

If you were a quantitative mathematics genius you would understand the meaning of words like "correlation coefficient" and "covariance." Correlation coefficient is a number that quantifies some type of statistical relationship between two or more variables or data values. Covariance measures the joint variability of two assets in a portfolio.

In the world of finance if ever two stocks might have identical price behavior (which is practically impossible!) one might say they have a correlation coefficient of 1 (perfectly correlated). Alternatively, two stocks with less similarity might have little or no correlation to each other and perhaps a correlation coefficient near to 0 (little or no correlation). In the unlikely scenario that the price of two stocks moved in identically opposite directions, then one could say they have a correlation coefficient of -1 (perfectly uncorrelated).

In building a portfolio there are two notable examples that might serve as an illustration of how to use the principle of correlation in your favor. One of the reasons for holding both stocks and bonds in a portfolio is that their correlation coefficient is not equal to 1. Estimates a few years ago put the correlation coefficient of stocks to bonds at approximately 0.60 (although it has become lower and lower over the past two decades—in fact, negative in the most recent decade. However, let's imagine a correlation coefficient of 0.60 exists between equities and bonds. It would mean

—— US Gov bonds vs Large Cap stocks, rolling 5yr correlation

5 year rolling correlations of monthly returns
Source: BofA Merrill Lynch Global Investment Strategy, Bloomberg, Ibbotson

Fig. 6.1   5 yr rolling correlations of US equities & government bonds

that when stock prices rise, let's say, 1.00%, then bond prices in the port-folio rise at a slower rate, 0.60%. The upside of bond holdings implied in this correlation coefficient will be that bond prices will rise at a slightly less robust rate than stocks.

However, when stock prices fall, one is likely to see less of a drop in bond prices. It is interesting to note that the correlation of bond prices to stock prices was moderately positive in the 1970s, 1980s, and 1990s. However, this trend has shifted in the new millennium and bond and equity prices have been negatively correlated during recent years. In the 1950s, 1960s, and in recent years, government bond prices have moved in the opposite direction to equity prices.

Another example of comparing correlation coefficient for two assets would be comparing the value of putting commodities, like gold, into a portfolio to cushion some equity exposure in your portfolio. On a stand-alone basis gold has seen some remarkable increases in price as well as some dramatic drops. However, traditionally gold has a low correlation coefficient with stock prices. It is estimated to be in the 0.20 range.

The popularity of hedge funds has grown dramatically over the past 20 years primarily owing to the guiding principle of correlation. Some of the more esteemed hedge fund managers make their living by promising that their performance results are "market neutral" and can make a profit no matter how volatile the stock or bond markets.

Understanding the Concept of Standard Deviation

Standard deviation as it relates to investing will help you understand the price volatility that occurs in almost every asset class. It is important to view every investment as something that is floating a bit in value sort of like a high tide and a low tide. There will always be a value or closing market price that can be attached to an asset at the end of each working day. However, prices fluctuate and the prices of certain assets fluctuate more than others. We commonly call such fluctuation by another word, volatility!

In most assets if we have recourse to a recent price history, we can normally predict within 68% certainty that the stock returns will be within a certain range (let's call it 1×). We can also predict within a 95% certainty that the return will be within a certain range (let's call it 2×). And we can also predict 99% of the time that asset performance will be within a certain range (let's call it 3×). Of course, there is always the spectre of the 1% occurring. Such rare events beyond the 3× or 1% range are what writer Nassim Nicholas Teleb in his 2007 book, "The Black Swan" has called the "Black Swan event." It is worth noting that when the hedge fund management firm based in Greenwich, Connecticut USA, Long Term Capital Management L.P., collapsed in the summer of 1998 it was explained by the founders and analysts as being a 500-year storm—that is, the result of the 1% occurring. After all the company had two Nobel Prize winners on its company board of directors. The collapse resulted in the firm registering losses exceeding USD 4.5 billion and essentially set off a severe correction in the global markets and resulting in widespread default on Russian debt, huge appreciation of the Japanese Yen, and near collapse of several economies in Southeast Asia.

	Arithmetic Mean (%)	Standard Deviation (%)
Large Company Stocks	12.1	20.2
Small Company Stocks*	16.9	32.3
Long-Term Corp. Bonds	6.3	8.4
Long-Term Govt. Bonds	5.9	9.8
Intermediate-Term Govt. Bonds	5.4	5.7
U.S. Treasury Bills	3.5	3.1
Inflation	3.0	4.1

The table above shows the mean return of US asset classes with the standard deviation (that is "volatility" or "risk") of those returns.

* The 1933 Small Company Stocks total return was 142.9%

Source: Bank of America- Merrill Lynch, Ibbotson

"In the long run, the higher the risk of the asset class, the higher the return."

Fig. 6.2

Bringing us back to the main point about standard deviation, let's remember that it measures the amount of variation from the average. This is an important term when it comes to assessing the investment potential of a stock or commodity or mutual fund or other type of asset. The riskier the asset the higher its standard deviation from its average is likely to be. Wise investors always calculate the reward versus the variability in price ratio.

	U.S. Lg Cap Growth	U.S. Lg Cap Value	U.S. Mid Cap Growth	U.S. Mid Cap Growth	U.S. Sm Cap Growth	U.S. Sm Cap Val	Foreign Industrialized Mkts Stocks	Emerging Mkts Stks	U.S. Investment Grade Bonds	U.S. High Yield Bonds	Non-U.S. Bonds	Cash	Commodities	Real Estate
U.S. Lg Cap Growth	1.000	0.848	0.896	0.740	0.856	0.718	0.582	0.517	0.189	0.528	0.005	0.023	0.124	0.444
U.S. Lg Cap Val	0.848	1.000	0.778	0.899	0.743	0.844	0.586	0.537	0.230	0.577	-0.008	0.052	0.141	0.588
U.S. Mid Cap Growth	0.896	0.778	1.000	0.776	0.980	0.792	0.558	0.559	0.125	0.562	-0.019	-0.019	0.162	0.515
U.S. Mid Cap Val	0.740	0.899	0.776	1.000	0.767	0.957	0.536	0.512	0.212	0.620	-0.015	-0.002	0.150	0.678
U.S. Sm Cap Growth	0.856	0.743	0.980	0.767	1.000	0.805	0.539	0.560	0.097	0.581	-0.036	-0.035	0.161	0.541
U.S. Sm Cap Val	0.718	0.844	0.792	0.957	0.805	1.000	0.516	0.517	0.160	0.644	-0.032	-0.013	0.157	0.701
Foreign Industrialized Mkts Stocks	0.582	0.586	0.558	0.536	0.539	0.516	1.000	0.667	0.170	0.398	0.288	0.052	0.181	0.389
Emerging Mkts Stks	0.517	0.537	0.559	0.512	0.560	0.517	0.667	1.000	0.036	0.432	0.025	0.003	0.201	0.343
U.S. Investment Grade Bonds	0.189	0.230	0.125	0.212	0.097	0.160	0.170	0.036	1.000	0.382	0.447	0.237	-0.107	0.157
U.S. High Yield Bonds	0.528	0.577	0.562	0.620	0.581	0.644	0.398	0.432	0.382	1.000	0.082	0.010	0.039	0.499
Non-U.S. Bonds	0.005	-0.008	-0.019	-0.015	-0.036	-0.032	0.288	0.025	0.447	0.082	1.000	0.229	-0.076	-0.001
Cash	0.023	0.052	-0.019	-0.002	-0.035	-0.013	0.052	0.003	0.237	0.010	0.229	1.000	-0.163	-0.050
Commodities	0.124	0.141	0.162	0.150	0.161	0.157	0.181	0.201	-0.107	0.039	-0.076	-0.163	1.000	0.159
Real Estate	0.444	0.588	0.515	0.678	0.541	0.701	0.389	0.343	0.157	0.499	-0.001	-0.050	0.159	1.000

Fig. 6.3

CHAPTER 7

Building an Investment Portfolio

Did You Know?
Dr. Harry Markowitz is considered by many to be one of the most influential figures in the history of asset management. Markowitz was born in 1927 and studied at the University of Chicago. He was fascinated with investment optimization techniques. A PhD dissertation essay he wrote in 1952 called "Portfolio Selection" later evolved into a book in 1958. It has been studied so extensively that it has become known as the definitive document on Modern Portfolio Theory (MPT). Markowitz was awarded the Nobel Prize in Economics in 1990.

So now you have arrived.

You understand the basic fundamentals of building an investment portfolio. So let's go for it! Let's push forward and build one.

BUILDING A CONSERVATIVE OR INCOME RISK PORTFOLIO

Often it is useful to start investing by being a bit conservative in regard to selecting individual securities in the portfolio and then gradually open up the levers to risk after one becomes more comfortable with the volatility in the market. A portfolio with the target of achieving an income stream should focus on preserving capital and controlling portfolio volatility.

© The Author(s) 2017

B. VonCannon, *A Guidebook for Today's Asian Investor*,

https://doi.org/10.1007/978-981-10-5831-8_7

Investor return within this type of risk profile is derived most often from the income generated from deposit or bond interest, and/or dividends from the underlying securities within the portfolio.

As such, using the asset allocation guidelines that we have spoken of earlier in this book, let's construct sections of the portfolio step by step.

First, we should decide to keep a portion of the investment funds liquid and we can call this portion the *Money Market/Cash segment* of the portfolio.

If we are investing in a US domestic booking center, we might be confined to investing only in US Dollar cash instruments. If one is investing in an offshore booking center outside of the United States, one might also be able to include more than US Dollar currency exposure in the portfolio. The sample seen below is a US Dollar reference currency portfolio—meaning the US Dollar is the yardstick currency against which the value of the portfolio is measured each year. If one lived in Amsterdam or Paris or Berlin, then one might select the Euro currency to be the reference currency. Or if one lived in London, the British Sterling might be the reference currency. Normally keeping up to 40–60% of a portfolio in the reference currency is considered a wise tactical decision. In times of extreme currency volatility like we experienced during or subsequent to crisis periods like those occurring in 1998 or 2008, one might consider keeping an even higher percentage of the portfolio assets denominated in the reference currency.

In this portion of the portfolio one should seek to place the cash assets in the safest possible type of investment. This would normally be a time deposit at a reputable bank. However, it could also be in a US Treasury bill. Treasury bills are debt instruments issued by the US government with maturities of 12 months or less. They are considered by most investment analysts to be the safest possible short-term investment instrument in the world today.

Next let's consider the *Fixed Income or Bond portion* of the portfolio. In the sample listed, this portion of the portfolio is approximately 50%. Within this portion one would also wish to diversify risk and this can be achieved by keeping limits on the exposure to any one debt instrument to no more than 5% of the portfolio. Also selecting the maturity of the bonds as well as a mix between government-issued debt and corporate-issued debt is considered wise investing.

Next let's consider the *Equity Portion* of the portfolio. Because the portfolio seeks to have low volatility and equity returns typically can be very volatile, then this section as a percentage of the overall investment portfolio is limited to 20% allocation within the total portfolio.

Again we seek diversification within this sector of the portfolio by select-ing equities from different geographical areas as well and diversifying between industries. You will note in this portfolio that 55% of the equities chosen are geographically based in North America and 40% of the equity exposure is to Euroland or Japan. A mere 5% is exposed to other global equity domiciles.

Beta Man Portfolio Management

US Dollar Global Income

Investment Profile

- Risk Profile: Income

- Time Horizon: 2 to 3 years

- Reference Currency: US Dollar

- Investment Objective: Capital Protection with preference for steady returns rather than high volatility in annual returns

Asset and Currency Allocation

Tactical Asset Allocation

ASSET CLASS	PERCENTAGE (%)
Cash	5
Fixed Income	50
Equities	20
Alternative Invst	25

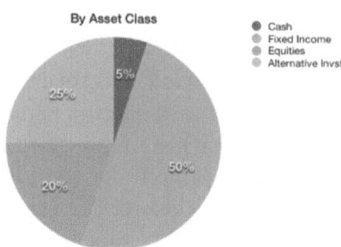

Currency Allocation

Currency Allocation

CURRENCY	PERCENTAGE (%)
US Dollar	84
AUD	6
Euro	5
JPY	5

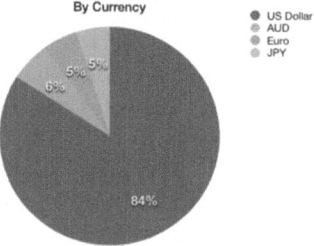

Equity: Geographical & Sector Allocation

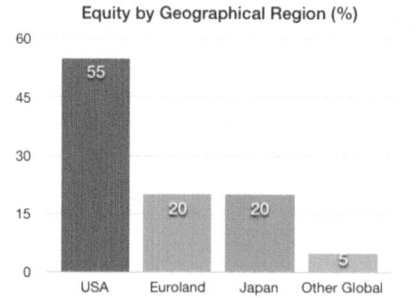

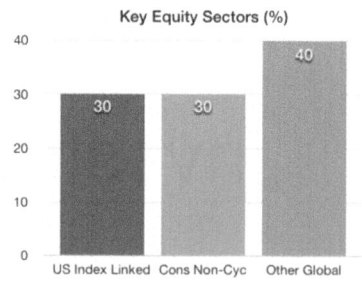

Global Income (USD 5mm)

Name/ Issuer	Description	Rating Moody's	Currency	YTM	Actual Price/ Rate	FX Rates	Value in USD	Percentage of Portfolio
CASH								
	Loc Curr Amt							
US Dollar	150,000					1.00	150,000	3%
Euro	46,296					1.08	50,000	1%
Yen	6,000,000					120.00	50,000	1%
AUD	0					0.71	0	
Total Cash							$250,000	5%
FIXED INCOME AND PREFERREDS								
JP Morgan High Yield Fun OHYFX	Bond Fund		USD		6.81	1.00	200,000	4%
Delaware Diversified Income A	Bond Fund		USD		8.58	1.00	200,000	4%
Oppenheimer Senior Floating Rate	Bond Fund		USD		7.57	1.00	200,000	4%
Aegon NV	Corporate	A	USD		27.87	1.00	100,000	2%
First Horizon Nat Corp	Corporate	A	USD		25.16	1.00	100,000	2%
First Rep Bk SF Cal D	Corporate	A	USD		24.89	1.00	100,000	2%
Maiden Holdings N Amer LT	Corporate	A	USD		27.22	1.00	100,000	2%
Metlife Inc	Corporate	A	USD		24.54	1.00	100,000	2%
Morgan Stanley	Corporate	BBB	USD		25.65	1.00	100,000	2%
Westpac Bkg Corp Floater 03/30/24	Corporate	AA	AUD	5.02	99.75	0.71	150,000	3%
Emirates NBD PJSC 4.75% 02/2022	Corporate	A	AUD	4.62	101.8	0.71	150,000	3%
Total Fixed Income							$2,500,000	50%

Name/ Issuer	Description	Rating Moody's	Currency	YTM	Actual Price/ Rate	FX Rates	Value in USD	Percentage of Portfolio
EQUITY								
SPDR S&P 500 ETF Trust	US Equities		USD			1.00	300,000	6%
Consumer Staples Select Sector SPDR Fund	US Equities		USD			1.00	300,000	6%
Wisdom Tree Eur Hedged Equity Fund	Euro Equities		USD			1.00	200,000	4%
Wisdom Tree Jpn Hedged Equity Fund	Jpn Equities		USD			1.00	200,000	4%
Total Equities							$1,000,000	20%
ALTERNATIVE								
Colchis P2P Income Fund	P2p Credit		USD			1.00	312,500	6.25%
Cumulus Fund	Power Supply		USD			1.00	312,500	6.25%
Athos Fund	M&A Fund		USD			1.00	312,500	6.25%
Segantii Asia-Pac Equity Multi Strat	Asian Multi-strat		USD			1.00	312,500	6.25%
Total Alternative							$1,250,000	25%
TOTAL PORTFOLIO						USD	$5,000,000	100%

BUILDING A BALANCED OR MODERATE RISK PORTFOLIO

Some investors seek higher returns but still like to keep volatility reduced to a moderate level. Investors of this ilk are often categorized as being in a Balanced Risk or Moderate Risk Portfolio investors. The key difference compared to the previous Income Risk Portfolio lies within the asset allocation adjustments.

We will start the **Money Market/Cash Portion** of the portfolio at a similar level to that of the previous Conservative Portfolio. Keeping a small amount of liquidity is always preferable in the case that cash is needed for some unforeseen reason. So we will place a 5% allocation into cash or money market in this portfolio.

Next we will build the **Fixed Income or Bond portion** of the portfolio. Compared to the Conservative or Income Risk Portfolio, the Balanced Risk portfolio will reduce the exposure in this portfolio to bonds to approximately 30% of the total portfolio. Nevertheless, the assets placed in this area of the portfolio should also be diversified a bit in order to reduce risk to any single issuer. You can see in the portfolio that no one bond position exceeds 4% of the overall portfolio. The issuers of the bonds also vary. Some of the bonds are corporate issues and some are government or quasi-government issues. The tenor of the bonds also is diversified. In this case the tenors of the bond portfolio range from 2 years to 10 years. As a matter of safety, most of the bonds in the portfolio have investment grade rating—that is their credit rating is at least BBB or higher (e.g. A, AA, or AAA).

Next let's construct the **Equity portion** of this balanced risk portfolio. The portfolio has a 75% geographical disposition toward North American equities. However, there is also geographical diversification in the portfolio as 15% is allocated to Euroland equity exposure and 5% to Japanese equities and another 5% to other international regions. In addition to mere geographical diversification, the portfolio also has diversification to more than one industrial sector. For example, you will note that 18% of the equity selection is to the consumer non-cyclical sector and 14% is allocated toward high tech equity exposure. Consumer cyclicals and financial stocks have 7% weighting each.

Our alternative portion of the portfolio has a 30% weighting and is diversified among four different selections.

The key point to remember when investing in alternative investments is that this area of the portfolio is intended to perform in a manner that may not be highly correlated with the equity markets. The alternative investment world includes hedge funds and they are typically divided into various categories. Most hedge fund managers pride themselves on being "market neutral," meaning that they are committed to being able to produce positive returns regardless of how the equity markets are trading. Thus, in down equity markets, they act as an insurance cushion offsetting weak equity market returns. In more buoyant equity market periods, hedge fund managers also promise investors that they will be able to produce positive returns. Hedge funds can be categorized in the following major categories.

Long-Short: an alternative fund that normally buys long equities that are expected to increase in value and while selling short equities that are expected to decrease in value.

Special Event: an alternative fund that seeks to exploit pricing inefficiencies that may occur before or after a corporate event such as bankruptcy, merger or acquisition, or spinoff.

Credit: an alternative fund whose underlying assets are chiefly in the form of credit-linked instruments.

CTF: an alternative fund whose underlying assets are related to "commodity-traded futures."

In recent years, analysts have also tended to include other types of specialty funds into the alternative investments category. Such types of investments might include commodity-linked investments or real-estate-linked investments. Again these are considered "alternative" owing to their weak or low correlation with the returns of the equity markets.

As far as building the positions in the Alternative Sector of your portfolio, it is wise to diversify and not put all the investment into one selection. It would be prudent to select a minimum of three or more types of alternative investment choices within your portfolio.

Beta Man Portfolio Management

US Dollar Global Balanced

Investment Profile

- Risk Profile: Balanced

- Time Horizon: 3 to 5 years

- Reference Currency: US Dollar

- Investment Objective: Moderate capital growth with preference for moderate returns rather than high volatility.

Asset and Currency Allocation

Tactical Asset Allocation

ASSET CLASS	PERCENTAGE (%)
Cash	5
Fixed Income	30
Equities	35
Alternative Invst	30

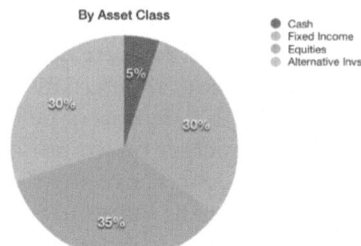

Currency Allocation

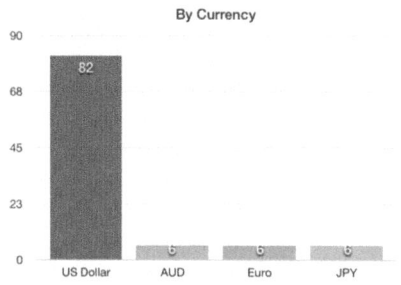

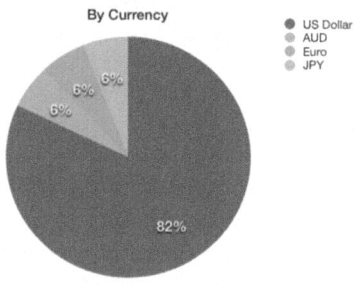

Equity: Geographical & Sector Allocation

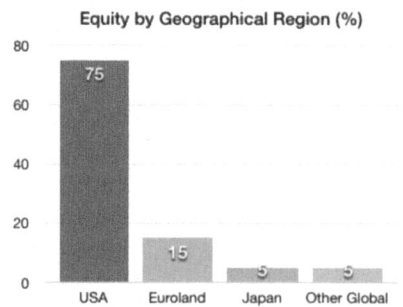

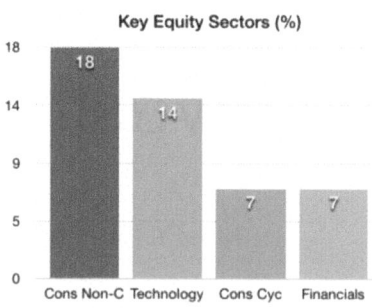

Global Balanced (USD 5 mm)

Name/ Issuer		Description	Rating Moody's	Currency	YTM	Actual Price/Rate	FX Rates	Value in USD	Percentage of Portfolio
CASH	Loc Curr Amt		Base Curr Amt					Value	Percentage(%)
US Dollar	250,000		250,000				1	150,000	3
Euro	46,296						1.08	50,000	1
Yen	6,000,000						120	50,000	1
AUD	0							0	
Total Cash								**$250,000**	**5**

FIXED INCOME AND PREFERREDS Issuer		Description	Rating Moody's	Currency	YTM	Actual Price/Rate	FX Rates	Value in USD	Percentage of Portfolio
JP Morgan High Yield Fund Select		Bond Fund		USD		7.17	1	200,000	4
Delaware Diversified Income A		Bond Fund		USD		8.65	1	200,000	4
Oppenheimer Senior Floating Rate		Bond Fund		USD		7.82	1	200,000	4
Aegon NV		Corporate	A	USD		27.87	1	100,000	2
First Horizon Nat Corp		Financial	A	USD		25.16	1	100,000	2
First Rep Bk SF Cal D		Financial	A	USD		24.89	1	100,000	2
Maiden Holdings N Amer LT		Corporate	A	USD		27.22	1	100,000	2
Metlife Inc		Financial	A	USD		24.54	1	100,000	2
Morgan Stanley		Financial	BBB	USD		20.65	1	100,000	2
Westpac banking Corp floating 03/03/24 YTM 5.02%		Financial	A	AUD	5.02	99.75	0.71	150,000	3
Emirates NBD PJSC 4.75% coupon 02/2022 YTM 4.3%		Financial	A	AUD	4.62	101.8	0.71	150,000	3
Total Fixed Income								**$1,500,000**	**30**

EQUITY Name/ Code		Description				Actual Price/Rate	FX Rates	Value in USD	Percentage of Portfolio
Nucor Corp	NUE	US Equities	Base Materials			40.11	1	62,500	1.25
BMW AG	BAMXY	Euro Equities	Consumer Disc			33.67	1	62,500	1.25
Coach Inc.	COH	US Equities	Consumer Disc			30.02	1	62,500	1.25
Mead Johnson Nutrition	MJN	US Equities	Consumer Non-D			81.24	1	62,500	1.25
Orkla AS	ORKLY	Euro Equities	Consumer Non-D			7.99	1	62,500	1.25
Proctor & Gamble Co	PG	US Equities	Consumer Non-D			74.66	1	62,500	1.25
Philip Morris Intl Inc	PM	US Equities	Consumer Non-D			84.02	1	62,500	1.25
TJX Cos Inc New	TJX	US Equities	Consumer Non-D			68.25	1	62,500	1.25
Citigroup Inc	C	US Equities	Financial			53.46	1	62,500	1.25
Willis Group Holdings Pub	WSH	UK Equities	Financial			43.83	1	62,500	1.25
Merck & Co Inc New	MRK	US Equities	Healthcare			53.03	1	62,500	1.25
Perkinelmer Inc	PKI	US Equities	Healthcare			50.68	1	62,500	1.25
CSX Corp	CSX	US Equities	Indust			27.05	1	62,500	1.25
Emerson Elec Co	EMR	US Equities	Indust			47.25	1	62,500	1.25
Pentair PLC	PNR	US Equities	Indust			54.45	1	62,500	1.25
Monmouth I RE	MNR	US Equities	Real Estate			10.67	1	62,500	1.25
Apple Inc	AAPL	US Equities	Tech			115.72	1	62,500	1.25
Cisco Sys Inc	CSCO	US Equities	Tech			27.83	1	62,500	1.25
EMC Corp Mass	EMC	US Equities	Tech			25.02	1	62,500	1.25
Fortinet Inc	FTNT	US Equities	Tech			33.27	1	62,500	1.25
Wisdom Tree Europe Hedged Equity Fu		Euro Equities	Global			53.03	1	250,000	5
Wisdom Tree Japan Hedged Equity Fun		Jpn Equities	Global			48.99	1	250,000	5
Total Equities								**$1,750,000**	**35**

ALTERNATIVE Name	Description			Actual Price/Rate	FX Rates	Value in USD	Percentage of Portfolio
Colchis P2P Income Fund	P2P Credit				1	375,000	7.5
Cumulus Fund	Power Suppl			862.71	1	375,000	7.5
Athos Fund	M&A Fund				1	375,000	7.5
Segantii Asia-Pac Equity Multi Strat	Asian Multi-S			386.77	1	375,000	7.5
Total Alternative						**$1,500,000**	**30**
TOTAL PORTFOLIO				USD		**$5,000,000**	**100**

BUILDING AN AGGRESSIVE OR GROWTH RISK PORTFOLIO

For investors who are experienced or who have a high level of risk tolerance, putting together a more aggressive or growth risk portfolio may be the best style of investing.

(Growth of a hypothetical USD 100,000 investment over the past 20 years)

Grew to	Asset Class	Avg Ann Returns (%)	Standard Deviation (%)
$494,958	Large Cap Value	8.3	15.2
$487,672	Small Cap	8.2	20.0
$439,531	Large Cap Core	7.7	15.3
$399,180	Diversified Portfolio	7.2	10.0
$378,545	Large Cap Growth	6.9	17.5
$280,442	Fixed Income	5.3	3.4
$226,366	International	4.2	16.9
$157,247	Cash	2.3	0.7

A Snapshot in Time: Asset Class Returns (1995 to 2011)

Main Asset Classes

	Returns	Volatility
Cash		
USD 3 month LIBOR	2.91%	0.67%
EUR 3 month LIBOR	2.04%	0.47%
Equities		
MSCI World Equity	2.82%	16.19%
S&P 500	3.93%	16.22%
DJ Eurostoxx 50	2.37%	20.42%
Nikkei 225	5.10%	19.58%
MSCI Emerging Markets	4.23%	25.15%
Fixed Income		
US Government Bonds 7-10 Years	6.54%	6.70%
European Government Bonds 7-10 Years	4.71%	4.66%
US Corporate Bonds	5.78%	6.89%
European Corporate Bonds 3-5 Years	3.81%	3.48%
Alternative Investments		
Hedge Funds	8.91%	7.65%
Real Estate	7.42%	18.37%
Commodities	1.89%	16.74%
Gold	9.52%	16.50%

In such type of portfolio the level of stock exposure will be higher. Over an extended time horizon, a carefully selected portfolio of stocks will outperform bonds and cash deposits.

However, it is also critical for the investor to understand that there is also a much higher level of volatility associated with investing in equities.

Now, as we start the Aggressive or Growth Portfolio, let's remember that it is prudent to allocate a bit of the portfolio to the Cash or Deposit Sector. In the example provided here, you will note an allocation of 5% to be kept highly liquid and in time deposit.

We will also allocate 12% for placing fixed income or bond portion into the portfolio.

More importantly in this more aggressive portion of the portfolio we will reduce exposure to Alternative Investments to a 13% allocation within the overall portfolio.

Our biggest adjustment compared to the prior two portfolios is to increase equity in the portfolio up 70%. Investors in this type of portfolio need to be reminded of the importance of having a long time horizon.

Among the equities to be placed into the portfolio they, too, should be diversified across country markets and region (by geography) and by across industrial sectors.

Finally, our positions in alternative investments should reflect a desire to keep portfolio performance intact. The beneficial aspect of adding alternative investments to any portfolio is, if they function properly as an asset, they will cushion the downward movement of a portfolio during poor equity market performing scenarios—sort of like an insurance policy! And during more buoyant equity market scenarios, they will be able to provide good returns, too.

Critics of hedge funds often malign the hedge fund community asserting that they charge costly fees to investors and they have unfavorable redemption policies. However, hedge funds often incur a cost for adding derivative positions to the portfolio. In the words of 1975 Nobel Prize winner Milton Friedman, **"There is no such thing as a free lunch."** Well managed hedge funds more often than not provide downside protection to the performance of the average investor.

Beta Man Portfolio Management

US Dollar Global Growth

Investment Profile

- Risk Profile: Growth

- Time Horizon: 4 to 6 years

- Reference Currency: US Dollar

- Investment Objective: Capital Growth with acceptable levels of volatility and even tolerance of negative growth periodically during the time horizon

Asset and Currency Allocation

Tactical Asset Allocation

ASSET CLASS	PERCENTAGE (%)
Cash	5
Fixed Income	12
Equities	70
Alternative Invst	13

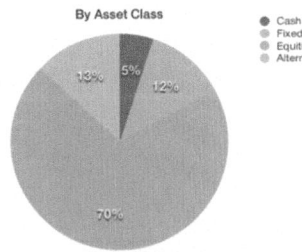

By Asset Class

● Cash
● Fixed Income
● Equities
● Alternative Invst

Currency Allocation

By Currency

CURRENCY	PERCENTAGE (%)
US Dollar	78
AUD	11
Euro	11

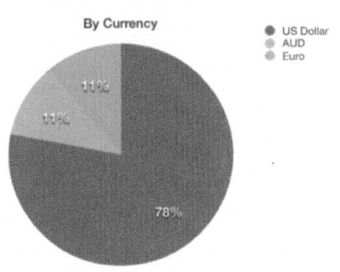

By Currency

● US Dollar
● AUD
● Euro

Equity: Geographical & Sector Allocation

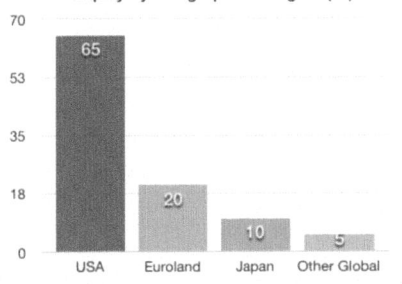

Equity by Geographical Region (%)

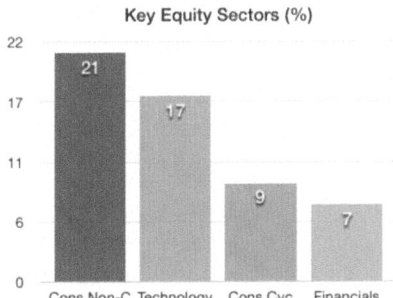

Key Equity Sectors (%)

Name/ Issuer	Description	Rating Moody's	Currency	YTM	Actual Price/Rate	FX Rates	Value in USD	Percentage of Portfolio
Global Growth (USD 5 mm)								
CASH								
	Loc Curr Amt							
US Dollar	150000					1.00	150,000	3%
Euro	46290					1.08	50,000	1%
Yen	6,000,000					120	50,000	1%
AUD	0						0	
Total Cash							$250,000	5%
FIXED INCOME AND PREFERREDS								
JP Morgan High Yield Fund Select	bond fund		USD			1.00	200,000	4%
Delaware Diversified Income A	bond fund		USD			1.00	200,000	4%
Oppenheimer Senior Floating Rate	bond fund		USD			1.00	200,000	4%
Total Fixed Income							$600,000	12%

EQUITY

Nucor Corp	US equities	Base Materi	USD	40.11	1.00	125,000	3%
BMW AG	Euro Equitie	Consumer Di	USD	33.67	1.00	125,000	3%
Coach Inc.	US equities	Consumer Di	USD	30.02	1.00	125,000	3%
Mead Johnson Nutrition Co	US equities	Consumer N	USD	81.24	1.00	125,000	3%
Orkla AS	Euro equitie	Consumer N	USD	7.99	1.00	125,000	3%
Proctor & Gamble Co	US equities	Consumer N	USD	74.66	1.00	125,000	3%
Philip Morris Intl Inc	US equities	Consumer N	USD	84.02	1.00	125,000	3%
TJX Cos Inc New	US equities	Consumer N	USD	68.25	1.00	125,000	3%
Citigroup Inc	US equities	Financial	USD	53.46	1.00	125,000	3%
Willis Group Holdings Public L	UK equities	Financial	USD	43.83	1.00	125,000	3%
Merck & Co Inc New	US equities	Healthcare	USD	53.03	1.00	125,000	3%
Perkinelmer Inc	US equities	Healthcare	USD	50.68	1.00	125,000	3%
CSX Corp	US equities	Industrials	USD	27.05	1.00	125,000	3%
Emerson Elec Co	US equities	Industrials	USD	47.25	1.00	125,000	3%
Pentair PLC	US equities	Industrials	USD	54.45	1.00	125,000	3%
Monmouth I RE MNR	US equities	Real Estates	USD	10.46	1.00	125,000	3%
Apple Inc	US equities	Technology	USD	115.72	1.00	125,000	3%
Cisco Sys Inc	US equities	Technology	USD	27.83	1.00	125,000	3%
EMC Corp Mass	US equities	Technology	USD	25.02	1.00	125,000	3%
Fortinet Inc	US equities	Technology	USD	33.27	1.00	125,000	3%
Wisdom Tree Europe Hedged Equity Fu	Euro equitie	Global	USD		1.00	500,000	10%
Wisdom Tree Japan Hedged Equity Fur	Jpn equities	Global	USD		1.00	500,000	10%
Total Equities						**$3,500,000**	**70%**

ALTERNATIVE

Colchis P2P Income Fund	P2P Credit	USD		1.00	162,500	3%
Cumulus Fund	Power supply	USD		1.00	162,500	3%
Athos Fund	M&A Fund	USD		1.00	162,500	3%
Segantii Asia-Pac Equity Multi-Strat	Asian Multi-strat	USD		1.00	162,500	3%
Total Alternative					**$650,000**	**13%**
TOTAL PORTFOLIO		USD			**$5,000,000**	**100%**

Before!   After!

Waiter: Your selection from the menu today, Monsieur?
Wilbur: We would like the Milton Friedman special!

CHAPTER 8

Understanding International Indices and Exchange Traded Funds

Did You Know?

The term "alpha" is often used in finance. It is in its simplest terms a measure of performance on a risk adjusted basis. Alpha measures the performance return of an investment relative to a market index which is used as a benchmark. It is particularly helpful in assessing mutual fund performance. The excess return of a fund or security relative to the return of a chosen benchmark index is what is often called the "alpha."

So now you understand the major asset classes! Let's navigate through the investment terrain!

Once you have a firm understanding of the major asset classes, that is money market products, fixed income and bond products, equities, and alternative investments like hedge funds, then you may move to a new level and try to understand how these products are sometimes packaged into other investment forms like exchange traded funds (ETFs) or index-linked products. With the continued development of the financial world in the past 20 years, it is worthwhile to know the geography of it.

Let's start first with the major securities market indices.

An index is a selection of securities which are representative of a country or region's market. Market indices vary in terms of what they represent. For example, a very broad index of stocks is the Russell 3000 (even broader in

© The Author(s) 2017

B. VonCannon, *A Guidebook for Today's Asian Investor*,

https://doi.org/10.1007/978-981-10-5831-8_8

numbers of stock than the S & P 500) or an index can be very limited in scope so as to represent something more specific like the MSCI Japan or the NASDAQ Biotechnology industry. The ways of constructing such an index can vary and the construction methodology and charter rules are normally decided by the index provider. The parties that make up an index are normally called its "constituents."

You may also wonder how indices are used. Here are three common uses of an index:

1. **It may serve as a barometer of a market's health and future course**. The S & P 500 and the FTSE 500 or the Hang Seng Index in Hong Kong all are normally used in any description of how the stock market in the United States and United Kingdom and/or Hong Kong are performing.
2. **Investment or asset managers may also use an index as a benchmark that helps to assess an investment manager's track record**. It is an investment manager's goal each year to outperform a benchmark that most closely resembles their style of investing.
3. **An index is also used for the intention of setting up an investment fund particularly when that fund purports to be a fund that tracks a particular index**. Many mutual funds and ETF fall into this category. An index fund manager would typically attempt to achieve a return for the investor that is close to representing the index.

World Indexes- Americas

INDEX	DESCRIPTION
Dow Jones Industrial Average	Founded in 1885, the Dow Jones Industrial Average is a price-weighted average of 30 blue chip stocks traded in the NYSE and NASDAQ
S&P 500 Index	S&P 500 Index is a capitalization-weighted index of 500 stocks. Because of its diverse constituency it is considered one of the best representations of the U.S. stock market and bellwether of U.S. economy
NASDAQ Composite Index	Founded in 1971 the NASDAQ Composite Index is a broad-based capitalization-weighted index of stocks in all three NASDAQ tiers that include Global Select, Global Market .Founded in 1971
RUSSELL 2000 index	Founded in 1984 the Russell 2000 index is composed of the 2000 smallest stocks in the Russell 3000 index and regarded in the industry as the premier measure of small-cap stock performance
S&P/Case-Shiller Home Price Indices	Using data dating back to 1890, this index is the leading measure for the US residential housing market tracking changes in the value of residential properties nationally as well as in 20 metro regions.
Mexican Stock Exchange Mexican Bolsa(IPC) Index	Founded in 1933 The Mexican IPC (also called "Mexbol" or " BMV" is a capitalization weighted index of the leading stocks traded on the Mexican Stock Exchange.
Bovespa Brazil Sao Paulo Stock Exchange Index	The index was set in 1968 for this barometer of the Brazilian economy. It is a gross return index weighted by traded volume and is comprised of about 50 stocks being the most liquid on the Sao Polo exchange

Fig. 8.1 The Major Global Indices

World Indexes- Europe, Africa, and Middle East

INDEX	DESCRIPTION
EURO STOXX 50 Price (Eur)	The Euro Stoxx 50 Index is a free-float market capitalization-weighted index of 50 European blue-chip stocks from those countries, participating in the European Community. Each component's weight is capped at 10% of the index's total free float market capitalization
FTSE 100 Index	The FTSE 100 Index is a capitalization-weighted index of the 100 most highly capitalized companies traded on the London Stock Exchange. An investibility weighting method is used for index calculation.
France CAC 40 Index	CAC stands for "Cotation Assistee en Continu" in French. It represents a capitalization-weighted measure of the 40 most significant values among the 100 highest market caps on the Euronext Paris exchange (formerly called the Paris Bourse)
Deutsche Borse AG (DAX)	The German Stock Index (normally called "The DAX") is a total return of 30 selected German blue chip stocks traded on the Frankfurt Stock Exchange. The equities use free float shares in the index calculation
Spain IBEX 35 Index	The IBEX is the official index of the Spanish Continuous Market. The index is comprised of the 35 most liquid stocks traded on the Continuous market.
FTSE MiB Index	The index consists of the 40 most liquid and capitalized stocks listed on the Borsa Italiana. In the FTSE MiB index foreign shares will be eligible for inclusion.
OMX Stockholm 30 Index	The OMX Stockholm 30 Index is a capitalization-weighted index of the 30 stocks that have the largest volume of trading on the Stockholm Stock Exchange. The equities use free float in index calculation.
Swiss Market Index	The Swiss Market Index is a capitalization-weighted index of the 20 larges and most liquid stocks on the Swiss Performance Index. It represents approximately 85% of the Swiss equity market.

World Indexes- Asia-Pacific

MSCI Asia Apex 50 Index	The MSCI Asia APEX 50 Indiex is a free float-adjusted, market capitalization weightered index. The index is a proxy for the MSCI Asia ex Japan Index, a benchmark index widely followed by investors investing in Asia
Japan Nikkei 225 Index	Calculated daily by the Nihon Keizai Shimbum (Nikkei) newspaper since 1950, it is a price weighted index of the top 225 Japanese companies listed in the First Section of the Tokyo Stock Exchange
Hong Kong Hang Seng Index	Started in 1969 by local Hong Kong owned bank, Hang Seng Bank, this index is a free-float capitalization weighted index comprised of selection of companies from the Stock Exchange of Hong Kong. The index is divided into four sub-indices: Commerce and Industry, Finance, Utilities, and Properties
Hong Kong Stock Exchange Hang Seng China Enterprises Index	The Hang Seng China Enterprises Index is a free float capitalization-weighted index is composed of H-Shares listed on the Hong Kong Stock Exchange and included in the Hang Seng Mainland Composite Index
Shanghai Stock Exchange Composite Index	The Shanghai Stock Exchange Composite Index is a capitalization-weighted index launched in 1991. This index tracks the daily price performance of all A-shares listed on the Shanghai Stock Exchange
Shenzhen Stock Exchange Component Stock Index	Dating to 1987 the Shenzhen Stock Exchange Component Stock Index is a capitalization weighted index The constituents consist of the 40 top companies that issue A-shares on Shenzhen Stock Exchange
Shanghai Shenzhen CSI 300 Index	The CSI 300 is a market capitalization weighted index which mirrors the performance of the 300 most highly liquid A-shares on the Shanghai and Shenzhen Stock Exchanges

Fig. 8.1 (Continued)

INDEX	DESCRIPTION
Taiwan Stock Exchange Weighted Index	First published in 1967 TAIEX is a capitalization-weighted index of all listed common shares traded on the Taiwan Stock Exchange
Mumbai Stock Exchange Sensex 30 Index	Published since 1986 the Sensex 30 is a capitalization-weighted index of 30 well-established and financially sound companies on Bombay Stock Exchange
FTSE Straits Times Index	Founded in 1966 the Straits Times Index (STI) is a capitalization-weighted stock market index tracking the performance of the top 30 companies listed on the Singapore Exchange
IDX Composite Index	Dating from the Dutch colonial government in 1912, the IDX today is the index tracking the stocks listed on the Indonesia Stock Exchange (formerly known as the Jakarta Stock Exchange)
Vietnam Securities Index (VSI)	Renamed VSI in 2009 this index is the first equity index that is composed of all of the stocks that are listed on the two exchanges in Hanoi and Ho Chi Minh City

World Indexes- Commodity

Dow Jones Precious Metals Index	Quoted in U.S. Dollars, the Dow Jones Precious Metals Index was created to represent the performance of U.S. trading stocks of companies engaged in gold, silver, and platinum production.
Dow Jones World Basic Materials Index	The Dow Jones World Basic Materials Index is an index consisting of companies which produce raw materials which are used to make finished or semi-finished products
FTSE Gold Mines Index	Launched in 1994 the FTSE Gold Mines Index Series reflects the performance of all gold mining companies that produce at least 300,000 oz/year and derive at least 51% of revenue from mined gold
MSCI World Energy Industry Group Index	The MSCI Energy Index is a capitalization weighted index that monitors the performance of energy stocks from around the world
MSCI World Materials Industry Group Index	The MSCI Material Index is a capitalization weighted index that monitors the performance of materials stocks from around the world
Wilderhill Clean Energy Index (ECO)	Launched in 2004 the ECO is a U.S. Dollar weighted index comprised of publicly traded companies whose businesses exist in order to benefit substantially from transition from alternative energies such as wind, solar, ethanol, and hydrogen fuel cells
S & P GSCI Index	The S & P GSCI Index serves as a benchmark for investment in the commodity markets and as a measure of commodity performance over time. It is a tradable index that is readily available for market participants of the CME. The index currently comprises 24 commodities from all commodity sectors- energy products, industrial products, agricultural products, livestock products, and precious metals

World Indexes- Fixed Income

INDEX	DESCRIPTION
Bloomberg Barclays US Aggregate Bond Index	It is a key market index for US bond investors. It is composed of four sub-indexes: US Government Index; US Credit Index; US Mortgage Backed Securities Index; and US Asset Backed Securities Index. The index holds investment grade bonds
Bloomberg Barclays Global Bond Index	Created in 1973 under the name of now defunct Lehman Brothers, the index provides a broad based measure of the global investment-grade fixed income markets. The three major components of the index are the U.S. Aggregate, the Pan-European Aggregate, and the Asian-Pacific Aggregate indices. The index also includes Eurodollar and Euro-Yen corporate bonds, Canadian government, agency and corporate securiteis, and USD investment grade 144A securities
Citigroup World Government Bond Index (Hedged and Unhedged)	The Citigroup World Government Bond Index is a market capitalization weighted index consisting of the government bond markets. Country eligibility is determined based on market capitalization and investibility criteria. All issues have a remaining maturity of at least one year
UBS Composite Bond Index	UBS Composite Bond Index is a market value weighted accumulation index of the UBS Government, Semi-Government, Corporate and Asset Backed Bond Indices. Return is figured as the sum of the market value weighted return of the individual sector indices
HSBC Offshore RMB Bond Index	The HSBC Offshore Renminbi Bond Index (CNH Index) tracks total return performance of Renminbi-denominated and Renminbi-settled bonds issued outside of China
JPMorgan Emerging Markets Bond Index	The J.P. Morgan Emerging Markets Bond Index is a total-return index that tracks the traded market for U.S. dollar-denominated Brady and other similar sovereign restructured bonds

Fig. 8.1   (Continued)

World Indexes- Other Major Indices

INDEX	DESCRIPTION
Baltic Dry Index	Dating back to London in 1823 the Baltic Dry Index (BDI) is a composite of Baltic Capesize, Panamax, Handysize, and Supramax indices. The index is designed as the successor to the Baltic Freight Index
Chicago Board Options Exchange Market Volatility Index (VIX)	VIX historical record dates back to 1990 and calculated by the Chicago Board of Options Exchange (CBOE). The index reflects a market estimate of future volatility, based on weighted average of the implied volatilities for a wide range of strike levels
U.S. Dollar Index	The U.S. Dollar index (USDX) measures the value of the United States dollar in comparison with six other major currencies including the Japanese Yen, Canadian dollar, Swiss franc, British Pound Sterling, Swedish Krona, and Euro
The Liv-ex Fine Wine 100 Index	Founded in 1999 the London International Vitners Exchange (Liv-ex) is an exchange for investment grade wine based in London and is the key industry benchmark. It represents the price movement of 100 of the most sought after fine wines for which there is a strong secondary market and is calculated monthly. The majority of the index consists of Bordeaux wines-----a reflection of the overall market---although wines from Burgundy, the Rhone, Champagne and Italy are also included
Deutsche Boerse World Luxury Index	The index base date began in 2007 and it comprises the 20 largest and most liquid issues of the luxury goods industry worldwide. A company is considered elligible if more than 50% of the overall turnover is generated from luxury products. The index constituents must have an average daily stock exchange turnover of at least USD 5 million to be elligible as well. The index weighting is based on market capitalization and each company is capped at 10% within the index weighting

Fig. 8.1 (Continued)

Such development and usage of indices in our daily financial world has spawned the development of global index providers who are typically used as "benchmarks" by ETF.

UNDERSTANDING ETFs

Exchange Trade Funds (or ETFs) are a category of investments that entered the financial scene about 25 years ago. During the 1990s new types of funds were developed with the intention of creating more cost efficient funds for average investors.

ETFs are open-end funds listed and traded on exchanges like stocks. ETFs allow investors to gain broad exposure to stock markets of different countries, emerging markets, sectors, and styles as well as fixed income and commodity. ETFs in recent years have enjoyed the reputation for providing more transparency than traditional funds as the managers provide the ETF portfolio composition to the market on a daily basis. ETFs also have some of the lowest expense ratios among registered investment products.

ETFs may include the following types of themes.

Equity themes:

Global capitalization (large, mid, small)
Sectors
Board markets

Emerging markets
Countries
Inverse/leveraged
Styles (like active, dividend, fundamental, infrastructure, real estate, shariah, thematic, private equity, value, growth)

Fixed income:

Government
Corporate
Credit
Inflation
High yield
Mortgage backed
Emerging markets

Currency:

Developed currencies
Emerging market currencies
Inverse/leveraged
Strategy (carry, momentum)

Cash:

Euro overnight index (EONIA)
Sterling overnight index (SONIA)
Fed funds

Alternatives:

Hedge funds
Carbon
Volatility

Commodities:

Broad based (S & P, GSCI, DJUBS, RICI, CRB)
Sub-indices (energy, livestock, precious metals, industrial metals, agriculture)

	Stocks	ETFs	Mutual Fund
Diversification	low	high	depends
Pricing	continuous	continuous	after mkt close
Liquidity	varies	higher	limited
Transparency	varies	higher	low
Fees	varies	lower	varies
Shorting	yes	yes	no
Limit Orders	Yes	Yes	No

Fig. 8.2 A Comparison between Stocks, ETFs, and traditional mutual funds. Source: Banque Privee Edmond de Rothschild

individual commodities
physical commodities (gold, silver, platinum, palladium)
Futures
Forwards
Inverse/leveraged

The structure of ETFs normally combines features of both stocks and index funds. In a manner similar to stocks, ETFs can be bought and sold on an exchange during trading hours, through any broker and on most trading platforms. And like index funds, ETFs contain baskets of securities designed to track specific indices. Some indices are narrow and may track a single market sector with fewer than a dozen holdings. Other indices can be much broader and include the entire market with thousands of holdings.

Below is a comparative listing of stocks, ETFs, and mutual funds. Kindly note the comparison of the three different asset types relative to diversification, pricing, liquidity, transparency, fees, the ability to short-sell the asset, and the ability to place limit orders.

A comparison between stocks, ETFs, and traditional mutual funds

The growth of ETFs in the past 15 years has been meteoric. In 2000, there was an estimated total of USD 75 billion invested in ETFs globally. Today that figure has grown to over USD 2.6 trillion. As of 2016, there were over 6000 ETF products in the market from nearly 277 providers and listed on over 64 market exchanges around the world. Of that USD 2.3 trillion, roughly 75% of the ETFs are equity theme ETFs. Fixed income accounts for about 15% of ETF themes and commodity and other investment themes account for about 5%. There are roughly 52 financial institutions today offering ETFs.

Roughly three major players in the global ETF market account for 72% of the Assets Under Management (AUM). They are i-Shares, State Street Global Advisors, and Vanguard. i-Shares, a firm owned by Blackrock Financial Group based in New Jersey (USA), is by far the largest accounting for almost 40% of the total market. The top ten ETF providers account for 86% of the total invested in ETFs. A list of the major ETF providers is found in Fig. 8.1.

| (AUM in USD billions) | | | Yr end 2016 | |
ETF Provider	Website	#ETFs	AUM	Mkt Share
I-Shares	www.ishares.com	700	1,030	38.3%
Vanguard	www.vanguard.com	200	473	17.6%
State Street	www.globalspdrs.com	146	439	16.3%
Powershares	www.investco.com	146	94	3.5%
Deutsche AWM	www.eft.db.com	213	66	2.5%
Lyxor AM	www.lycoretf.com	172	51	1.9%
Wisdom Tree	www.wisdomtree.com	94	49	1.8%
Nomura Asset Mgmt	www.nextfunds.jp	37	48	1.8%
ETF Securities	www.etfsecurities.com	260	37	1.4%
Ch. Schwab	www.schwab.com	200	30	1.1%
Others	-			14.0%
Total Market:			2,692	

Fig. 8.3   Major Players of Global ETF Market. Source: Citywire Asia/Deutsche Bank (2015)

"Honey, you watch Hong Kong, I'll watch London Footsie, and the cat will wake up when New York opens."

Fig. 8.4 In Today's Digital Age, equity trading occurs virtually around the clock

CHAPTER 9

Understanding Benchmarking

Did You Know?
One of the most widely used benchmarks in the world today is the Morgan Stanley Composite World Index (USD). It was started in 1969 and captures the stocks of large- and mid-cap companies spreading over 23 countries with over 1600 constituents. It is considered to represent 85% of the market capitalization in each country.

Part of undertaking a wise investment decision process is setting realistic expectations. Choosing a benchmark against which to assess your investment portfolio's annual success can be most helpful. It will help you remain unflustered during times when there is volatility in the market and you wish to assess your portfolio performance. One should always seek to find the "best of breed" when seeking an investment.

Now you may be asking why all the fuss about benchmarking. Why do financial analysts use benchmarks? The answer is that it helps one to determine how their investments are performing vis-à-vis competitors or in relationship to other funds or assets holdings of similar risk category. One often hears the saying "Don't compare apples to oranges!" Benchmarking follows a similar philosophy. It is unfair to compare the performance of an emerging market stock fund to a blue chip US large-cap stock fund. The emerging market stock fund will most likely have a high level of volatility and would be best compared to a batch of other emerging market funds or an emerging market index. The blue chip US large-cap fund would be likely benchmarked to another large cap or a large-cap index. Comparing stock funds to a bond fund index or money market index would also not be such an ideal metric for comparison. They are different asset classes.

One of the most widely used benchmarks is the Morgan Stanley Composite Index (MSCI) which is a selection of blue chip stocks on the NYSE who trade actively and are widely considered to be industry leaders in their respective industries.

Another benchmark that is popular in Europe is the Eurostoxx 50 which is a selection of blue chip European shares. Still another popular benchmark is the FTSE 500 which is a selection of the blue chip names from the United Kingdom's stock market.

One of the buzz words that became widely used in the financial community a few years ago was the label "absolute return," that is a performance target or destination which seeks to maximize the return without regard to a set benchmark. Whereas calling something an "absolute

Fig. 9.1 A visit to your local private banker begins with a discussion on setting realistic investment expectations! Avoid setting unrealistic expectations like this client, "I want 20% annual return with capital protection and no risk"

(AUM in USD billions)			Yr End 2011	
Index provider	Website	#ETFs	AUM	Pct of total
S&P	www.standardandpoors.com/indices	387	315	23.3%
MSCI	www.mscibarra.com	486	304	22.5%
Barclays Capital	www.barcap.com/indices	108	146	10.8%
STOXX	www.stoxx.com/html/indices	288	87	6.4%
Russell	www.russell.com/indexes	100	78	5.8%
FTSE	www.ftse.com/indices/index.jsp	171	53	3.9%
Dow Jones	www.djindexes.com/	170	53	3.9%
Markit	www.markit.com/en/	131	51	3.8%
NASDAQ OMX	www.indexes.nasdaqomx.com/	64	35	2.6%
Topix	www.tse.or.jp/english/	55	17	1.3%
Nikkei	www.e.nikkei.com/e/fr/markelive.asp	12	18	1.3%
NYSE Euronext	www.nyse.com	44	16	1.2%
Hang Seng	www.hsi.com.hk/HIS-Net/	14	13	1.0%
Wisdom Tree	www.wisdomtree.com	35	10	0.7%
EuroMTS	www.euromtsindices.com/	32	6	0.5%

Fig. 9.2 Global Index providers used as benchmarks by ETFs. Source: Banque Privee Edmond de Rothschild

return fund" or using "absolute return" to describe a performance target sounds impressive, in the end, the performance results of many "absolute return funds" are compared to some sort of target or commonly used criteria for assessing performance. The acid test is really does the fund perform or not. The hedge fund world is defined by absolute returns. Absolute return fund managers are in large part characterized by their use of short selling, leverage, and high turnover of product in their portfolios.

APPLYING THE CONCEPT OF BENCHMARKING TO YOUR INVESTMENT PROCESS

A benchmark is a yardstick for measuring investment success or failure. It is a method that shows the average performance of a specific set of securities. Benchmarks may be modeled after published indices or specially tailored to fit a specific type of investment strategy. Benchmarks are the standard by which you should judge the performance of individual assets in your portfolio. They also allow you to evaluate your portfolio as a whole. It is difficult to fully evaluate the success of an investment portfolio without having a benchmark against which to compare the portfolio.

Benchmarks generally serve three basic purposes.

First, they allow the investor to track the average returns of a specific asset class.

Second, benchmarks may allow the investor to compare different fund managers operating in similar asset classes. They also allow the investor to follow the recommendations that may have been made by a financial advisor.

Third, benchmarks provide useful fundamental base for allowing the investor to construct new portfolios and ETFs.

These considerations may also figure into the investor's selection of the appropriate benchmark:

- Is the proposed benchmark representing the type of assets that interest the investor?
- How wide and deep is the benchmark? Is it broadly defined?
- How many different types of securities are listed within the benchmark?
- What generally constitutes the benchmark and how is it put together?
- How is the benchmark weighted?

Benchmarks are generally divided into categories based on type, geography, size, industry, investment style, and possibly the maturity of a given type of financial asset.

Here is what I am talking about.

Benchmark by Type

Benchmarks may be categorized by type of financial asset: stock, bonds, and other asset classes.

Stock benchmarks are generally subdivided by market capitalization, geography, industry, and investment style.

Bond benchmarks are generally subdivided into corporate bonds, government bonds, convertible bonds, agency bonds, municipal bonds, and junk bonds.

Each asset class defines its own benchmarks. Therefore you might see real estate investment trusts (REITs), currencies, commodities, derivatives, gold, and hedge funds each have their own benchmarks.

Benchmark by Geography

They may be categorized by the following.

Global benchmarks: they measure the performance of assets in several developed market countries, including the United States. A notable example of this type of benchmark might be the MSCI World and/or MSCI All Country Free.

International benchmarks: they measure the performance of assets in mostly developed countries outside of the United States. Some notable examples of such international benchmarks might be MSCI Europe, MSCI Australia, and MSCI Far East Index.

Emerging market benchmarks: they measure the performance of assets in the emerging market world which would generally include Asia, Latin America, Emerging Europe, and South Africa. Some notable examples might include the S&P/IFC Emerging Market Free Index and the MSCI Emerging Markets Free index.

Regional benchmarks: they help the investor keep track of the performance of assets in a specific region of the world. Some notable examples might include MSCI Europe, MSCI Asia, Dow Jones Asia, and Dow Jones Latin America.

Country benchmarks: they measure the performance of assets in a specific country. Some notable examples of country benchmarks might include the S & P 500, the Russell 5000, Dow Jones, MSCI Argentina, MSCI Chile, Straits Times Index (in Singapore), and Japan TOPIX.

Asset Size: benchmarks may also be placed in category by size and market capitalization is probably the most common form of categorizing by size. As such market capitalization benchmarks measure the performance of assets within a given range of capitalization. Here would be a breakdown of some commonly used market cap ranges:

Large cap: Stocks of companies with market cap exceeding USD 10 billion

Mid cap: Stocks of companies with market cap USD 2 billion to USD 10 billion

Small cap: Stocks of companies with market cap US Dollar less than USD 2 billion

Micro cap: Stocks of companies with market cap less than USD 250 million

Industry: industry benchmarks are also sometimes called "sector benchmarks" and they measure the performance of assets in a specific industry, such as telecommunications, financial services, retail, automotive, or consumer durables. Industry benchmarks may also be subcategorized by geography. For example, there are industry benchmarks for specific areas like the European automotive industry or the Chinese telecommunications industry.

Investment Style: it is common today to refer to stock investing in terms of value stocks or growth stocks. Accordingly, investment style benchmarks can measure the performance of stocks within these styles. Typically a value benchmark might measure the performance of stocks that are considered to be undervalued by the market. As such their P/E ratios are lower than the average P/E and Price to Book ratios for all companies. Another example of an investment style benchmark might be a growth benchmark that measures the performance of stocks that are expected to have accelerated growth caused by increased earnings or other factors like superior market position. Growth benchmark stocks might have P/E and Price to Book ratios that are higher than the average P/E and Price to Book ratios for all companies. Other types of investment benchmarks might exist, too. A blend benchmark normally refers to the performance of a set group of stocks which might consist of both value and growth stocks.

Maturity: categorizing by asset maturity is also a method of benchmarking and quite popularly applied to the bond markets. For example, a long-term bond benchmark might apply to bonds that have a maturity exceeding ten years. A benchmark for bonds maturing within two to ten years might be labeled an intermediate-term benchmark.

Assessing the Usefulness of Benchmarks

Normally a good benchmark should encompass the following qualities.

Clear and transparent: There should be no doubt as to the names of the securities in the benchmark and their relative weighting within the benchmark.

Investment access: The benchmark should include securities that can actually be purchased in the market.

Pricing: Daily available

Historical data: Should be available so as to measure historical returns.

Low turnover: Within the context of the index there should not be high turnover of securities in the index as it would present difficulties for investors' asset allocation decisions.

Prior specification: Benchmarks should be in existence prior to the beginning of the period of evaluation.

Risk metrics: Should be published regularly for the benchmark so that investment managers can compare current portfolio risks with the known benchmark risks.

In the final analysis choosing a benchmark is an important aspect of measuring investment performance.

The selection of benchmark should be compatible with the investment strategy of the investment portfolio.

CHAPTER 10

Investing in the Future: The Glass Is Half Full

"I see trees of green, red roses too
I see them bloom for me and you
And I think to myself what a wonderful
world"
—Lyrics from Louis Armstrong song, "What a Wonderful World"

Sometimes reviewing history can help us understand the present as a part of a current or passing trend. What I have observed in the past 30 years in the financial industry is that markets continuously change and financial products continuously evolve. I like to make reference to the "Exocet missle analogy." Most adults who were living during the brief 1982 war between Argentina and the United Kingdom over the Falkland Islands will remember the devastating effect of the new Exocet missle technology which, when the missile was launched, seem a real game changer in war technology. Financial products today really have no Exocet missle—that is a product that when developed is so special that when you have it, nobody can compete with you. Whatever product a bank or financial institution may develop, its market advantage is ephemeral and likely only a matter of months before other competitors will be offering a similar product at the same or cheaper price. Essentially the color of money is the same at all banks. (Note: And by the way, the Exocet missile, too, was eventually replaced by more sophisticated and deadlier air-to-target missile defense weaponry.)

© The Author(s) 2017
B. VonCannon, *A Guidebook for Today's Asian Investor*,
https://doi.org/10.1007/978-981-10-5831-8_10

There is a broader trend today in financial markets that has been gaining in velocity the past 30 years since the fall of the Berlin Wall and evolving new technology in the workplace has been its engine. The world has become linked and connected like never before. For better or worse, increasingly we now live in a global village. As much as many in our society today would like to turn back the clock and go back in time, it cannot be. Today information and money travel at the speed of sound.

Some historians and analysts believe the global village period that started with the fall of the Berlin Wall in 1989 ended during the Great Financial Crisis (GFC) of 2008. While the gap between rich and poor and other social ills are today are perhaps more (not less) acute, I believe the lessons learned in 2008 were very valuable and one day the GFC will be viewed as a blip in financial history—a temporary pause.

Given this backdrop I think there are a few key trends that will emerge in the coming 25 years.

CONTINUED GLOBALIZATION OF INVESTMENT CHOICES

I often mention the Berlin Wall when talking at seminars about financial history. This event in 1989 greatly accelerated globally investing. Prior to that date, the world was still entrenched in the old trading blocs built up during the Cold War, a period extending back to the end of World War II in 1945. During the Cold War period the world was divided mainly between two trading blocks, the capitalist world including the United States and its allies in Western Europe and Asia, and, juxtaposed, the communist world including the Soviet Union and Eastern Europe and China. While there was some trade in between the two blocks of nations, it was rather limited by today's standards.

The fall of the Berlin Wall in late 1989 essentially broke down that paradigm and created a new world order within which almost unlimited possibilities could advance in global trade. In the real economy globalization has helped to keep consumer prices in most developed countries much lower than they would have otherwise been. In the financial world, globalization has accelerated the pace and depth with which one can participate in investment opportunities across the globe. Freer access to capital has fueled, not stymied, development of the emerging economies of the world.

Today there are many avenues by which one can gain access to an attractive investment opportunity on the other side of the globe. It could be through the direct investment in a foreign currency or in a foreign stock market. It could be through an American Depository Receipt (also known as "ADR") listing of a foreign company on the NYSE or NASDAQ. We used to joke in the investment community the best way to take advantage of the economic boom in China in the 1990s was to buy Mercedes Benz stock. Why? Because at the time it was very difficult to invest directly into the China stock market but Mercedes sold so many of its cars to the new millionaires being created in China. So the logic went that to buy a share of Mercedes stock was tantamount to investing in the China market!

Fig. 10.1 Treat your portfolio as if growing your money. Adopt a proper time horizon and keep a disciplined asset allocation

At the time of printing this book, we have witnessed in recent months the manifestation of some nascent anti-globalization political movements (also referred to as "populist" or "nativist" movements) springing up across the globe. Most notably in 2016 the outcome of the Brexit vote in the United Kingdom, the surprising election of "anti-establishment" candidate Donald Trump as US President, and the failed Italian referendum by Prime Minister Renzi are events that have shocked the modern world. There are extreme view political candidates on the right and the left of the political spectrum who are preaching that less (not more) openness in trade and access to global markets should be adopted. Gaps in income equality across the globe in both developed and underdeveloped countries have exacerbated views on the benefits of free global trade. It is easy to empathize with points of logic raised by those who are doubting the merits of free trade and globalization.

However, I tend to find greater sympathy for those who see the merits of new technology and the global village. The globalization trend of the past 25 years has brought us improvements in health standards and eradicating disease around the globe, more awareness of environmental issues, and increased educational standards in both developed and underdeveloped countries. If we can remember the tenets of "comparative trade theory," we can also see there is more good than bad. Such theory dates to early nineteenth century England and the classical economist writer David Ricardo who espoused that, when applied in government policies in proper dosage and over a gradual amount of time, free and open trade results in citizens of a country potentially benefiting from greater availability of goods and services at the most fair and convenient price points. It is possible that both rich and poor benefit from free trade policies. History shows that countries that practice free trade are usually wealthy countries. We may go through some bumps in the road in the coming decade debating how trade policies can be better implemented. However, the 1930s and the wars that followed should teach us that protectionism does not make us richer. It lowers the level of wealth for everyone. It is for this reason that over the longer term in the coming quarter century, I predict that the forces of globalization will be unstoppable and will triumph over the current wave of xenophobia and protectionist mindset that is sweeping the globe. For the investor, open and free markets allow capital (often coming from investors like you and me) to place family wealth in ideas and product innovations and companies that are offering just reward for the entrusted capital. Restricting investment flows inhibits innovation and performance; in countries that practice rigid protectionism, it rewards pampered and preferred industries rather than those who truly deserve it and can offer best return on capital.

Continued Proliferation of Hi-tech Investment Gadgetry that Brings Information to the Individual Investor

In the old days one gathered information on the financial markets from daily newspapers, watching a TV show, listening to a radio report, or (if one had access to it) a telex machine ticker tape. One might have picked up a copy of Financial Times or Wall Street Journal over a morning coffee. One might have relied on an occasional meeting with a financial advisor. However, information on the markets today is continuously available 24/7 on smartphone gadgets that can fit in a suit pocket or hand purse. There is a market open and accessible for trading somewhere in the world every hour of the day. Furthermore, one can increasingly access such markets from one's smartphone. The efficiency and ease with which one can have access to markets is improving daily. Today anyone who has a thirst for knowledge and information about financial goods and services can prosper; everyone has potential to become an expert.

The second area of technology that is having a significant impact on the financial markets is the growing phenomenon of high frequency trading and algorithmic trading and artificial intelligence (A.I.). These are trading platforms usually controlled by highly sophisticated and well-financed groups or individuals whose research and information databases give it a significant advantages over the investment platform of the average investor. These new trading platforms have fallen under the watchful glare of regulators in many developed countries. It is not uncommon to see them trading many thousands of shares daily and moving constantly in and out of the market trying to realize quick profits. Performance statistics suggest that some of these groups are capable of offering good returns to investors. However, the jury is still out on such type of investing. Temporary suspensions or complete shutdown of trading in certain country markets owing to power outages or sabotage seems to be happening more frequently as the years pass. Whether or not these disruptions will make such type of trading unwise or represent a major threat to the integrity of our financial markets is under review by regulators, scholars, and analysts.

Fig. 10.2 The Age of Beta Man: "Continued proliferation of hi-tech investment gadgetry brings information to the individual investor!"

Continued Threat of Global Conflicts and New and Different Market Risks

Sadly our world has had conflicts since Adam ate the apple and got involved with Eve. Resentments that lead to conflicts between ethnic and religious groups and nation states have also been around since Cain knocked off Abel. This is a category of unknown knowns. We may not know where and when it will happen but we know there will be future conflicts; it is the nature of mankind.

It is a good idea to plan one's investing activities always expecting that violence ranging from terrorist activity to outright invasion of land sovereignty could occur and will not stop in our lifetimes. If anything, it is a good reason why it is important continue to diversify one's wealth across asset classes. Remember no single asset class performs the best every year.

Greater Effort by All Governments to Collect Taxes and Erect Tax Compliance Legislation

I have been a proponent of flat tax rate most of my adult life. Taxes are a necessary part of life. We need roads. We need bridges. We need public schools and a police force to enforce basic public security. We also need some form of government to administer all of this at a local, regional, and national level. Most countries also need to fund an army to provide defense of their territorial integrity in the face of threats from abroad. It has been my hope that more governments will learn to operate within a budget and record maybe even a slight surplus. However, this seems almost utopic in thought given the poor track record of most governments to collect taxes against its populations in a fair and equitable manner.

Tax loopholes need to be reviewed and limited, too. Tax rates are so high today, in my view, partly because in many countries in the developed world there are loopholes that allow many smart and/or well-advised persons with adequate financial means to afford accountants and lawyers to seek out the loopholes. As a result, increasingly it is the average person or middle class that is being forced to shoulder the burden of providing tax revenues. If we had a flat tax rate and limitations on tax loopholes, everybody would have "skin in the game" and be forced to contribute toward keeping our government budget revenues more robust.

Governments today around the world have also become more desperate in their attempts to collect taxes. The US government has been one of the few governments that attempts to collect taxes from its citizens who live overseas. The manner in which they have attempted to collect these taxes through laws like the recent Foreign Account Tax Compliance Act (commonly called "FATCA") legislation in the United States is increasingly encroaching on the right to individual privacy and has damaged the United States' reputation in the global business and financial communities around the world. Furthermore, a more recent set of global guidelines set up by the OECD Council, called Common Reporting Standard (commonly referred to as "CRS") initiative aims to set up an automatic exchange of tax and financial information on a global level. To date the central government of over 100 nations (not including the USA) have supported and signed an agreement to fully implement these CRS requirements.

All investors should be aware of growing effort by all governments through dual taxation treaties, the new CRS agenda, and other agreements to collect more taxes.

CONTINUED OPPORTUNITIES TO GROW ONE'S WEALTH!

In the future financial market trading volume around the world is positioned to grow by quantum proportions simply because there will be a larger audience of people with both the wealth and access to gadgets that allow access to the financial markets. I cite two factors which I think will propel the world forward toward greater wealth accumulation.

First, we will see continued growth and development in the emerging markets. Today ten countries hold approximately 72% of the world's GDP. While there will always be a top ten and they might hold a disproportionate percentage of global wealth, I predict that emerging market countries will increasingly comprise a larger portion of global GDP. Obviously this depends on continued evolution in political leadership and democratization of poorer societies so that middle classes can develop in underdeveloped and developing nations. It also depends upon a responsible spirit and policies among developed countries that promotes free and fair trade as well. The burden of responsibility is not merely on leadership of smaller, poorer nations. The political leadership of large, wealthier nations is critical, too. The early hints of adopting "jingoist trade policies" emanating from the early days of the Trump Administration are cause for great concern. It appears at odds with the affluence and global political influence gained by the United States during the past 100 years which has been built largely upon a policy anchored by the principle of open markets and knocking down obstacles to free and fair trade. Lest we not forget that the preeminent global power just over 100 years ago was Great Britain (not the United States). Going forward we cannot just assume or take for granted that the United States will maintain is prominent role if its economic policies degenerate and its diplomatic behavior abdicates global leadership responsibility.

Second, there will be a dramatic increase in the number of people investing in the financial markets. Consider this fact: China today has about 22% of the global population. However, in China less than 15% of its 1.4 billion population have investment exposure to the stock market. This contrasts markedly with the United States where roughly 40% of the population have investment exposure to the stock market and in France where the figures is just under 20%. While participation levels by percentage of population in their own stock market by Chinese citizens may not reach the same level as the United States overnight, it is quite likely that the percentage will increase significantly in the years ahead. Bear in mind that for every 1% additional exposure to the financial markets in China, that is 14 million new families participating in the market. If one factors in India where participation rates in the market are also exploding with growth amongst its population of 1.3 billion, there is likely to be exponential growth in the number of participants in the Bombay Stock Exchange. The same can be said for the 608 million people who live in the ASEAN countries in Southeast Asia.

If not for other reasons, these are valid reasons for staying informed about what is happening in the global financial markets. Perhaps 50 years ago one could not possibly study and know a lot about the financial markets unless one had access to a large library in one's neighborhood. One might not have had the family connections or luxury of knowing a good financial advisor. However, today everyone can become knowledgeable about investing. Everyone has the potential to become an expert. You can grow your own money tree both literally and figuratively. Through the use of internet search engines and knowing how to operate computer tablets and smartphones one can have access to learning about the financial markets through mere desire and self-discipline to engage in such study.

Fig. 10.3 "Everyone has the potential to become a financial expert!"

Fig. 10.4 The Money Tree: *Crassula ovata (latin)*—a succulent form of tree plant native to South Africa or Mozambique seasonably adorned with pink or white flowers and commonly known by the name of "money tree"

INDEX

© The Author(s) 2017
B. VonCannon, *A Guidebook for Today's Asian Investor*,
https://doi.org/10.1007/978-981-10-5831-8

The manufacturer's authorised representative in the EU is Springer
Nature Customer Service Centre GmbH, Europaplatz 3, 69115 Heidelberg,
Germany. If you have any concerns regarding our products, please
contact ProductSafety@springernature.com

Printed and bound by CPI Group (UK) Ltd, Croydon, CR0 4YY
29/04/2026
02099460-0003